PSYCHIC PHENOMENA

Also by Willard A. Heaps

Assassination: A Special Kind of Murder
Birthstones
Juvenile Justice
Long Journeys: Stories of Human Endurance
Riots, U.S.A.
The Story of Ellis Island
Superstition!
Taxation, U.S.A.
Wall of Shame
Wandering Workers: The Story of American Migrant Workers and Their Problems

With Porter W. Heaps

The Singing Sixties; The Spirit of Civil War Days Drawn from the Music of the Times

PSYCHIC PHENOMENA

by

Willard A. Heaps

THOMAS NELSON INC., PUBLISHERS
Nashville New York

Published in Nashville, Tennessee, by Thomas Nelson Inc. and simultaneously in Don Mills, Ontario, by Thomas Nelson & Sons (Canada) Limited. Manufactured in the United States of America.

First Edition

Library of Congress Cataloging in Publication Data
Heaps, Willard Allison
Psychic phenomena.

Bibliography: p.
Includes index.
1. Psychical research. I. Title.
BF1031.H3 133.8 74-10266
ISBN 0-8407-6418-9

Acknowledgments

The author is grateful for the assistance of many specialists and librarians who have made suggestions for the treatment of specific subjects in this book, and to the following authors and publishers for quoted material: the late Eileen Garrett, *Adventures in the Supernatural* (Garrett-Helix); Arthur Koestler, *The Roots of Coincidence* (Random House); J. Gaither Pratt, *ESP Research Today* (Scarecrow Press); Louisa Rhine, *ESP in Life and Laboratory* (Macmillan); Joseph B. Rhine, *The Reach of the Mind* (Morrow); Joseph B. Rhine and J. Gaither Pratt, Parapsychology (C. C. Thomas); Harold Sherman, *Your Mysterious Powers of ESP* (World); and Ian Stevenson, *Telepathic Impressions* (University of Virginia Press).

In addition,the writings of Melbourne Christopher, Herbert B. Greenhouse, Renée Haynes, Hans Holzer, George Kreskin, Lawrence LeShan, and Susy Smith have proved valuable. The Foundation for Research on the Nature of Man (formerly the Duke University Parapsychology Laboratory) has supplied several cases from its files.

Thanks are due also to the British periodical *Light*, and to *Mademoiselle* and *Science* for quotations from some of their articles.

CONTENTS

PSYCHIC PHENOMENA

CHAPTER 1

Psychic Powers

While he was on shipboard, a sailor suffered a slight injury to one shoulder, and his arm was put in a cast to speed up the recovery. To avoid worrying his family, he was careful not to mention the matter in any of his letters home. But his mother wrote to him and asked why he hadn't told them that his shoulder was hurt and his arm in a cast.

"I lived fourteen miles from Memphis, Tennessee. One day I went to town to see a movie. I had an uneasy feeling as I entered the movie that something was on fire at home. This feeling grew until I could endure it no longer. I left the movie with an overpowering pull that drove me homeward.

"Within a mile of home I saw the fields all black and smoking. A boy hunting rabbits had thrown a lighted match in a field and started a fire. It took the fire department and fifty volunteers to save my home.

"Was this ESP?"

While a married couple was on a cross-country trip

by car, the wife awoke one morning and asked her husband if he would please drive very carefully that day. She said she had dreamed that a highway patrol car had suddenly pulled out from a side road on the right and crossed just in front of them into the center lane of the highway. She had awakened from the dream before any collision occurred, but with a feeling of real danger.

The event the wife reported occurred the next day just as she had foreseen it in her dream. The husband wrote that his wife's description of the direction the patrol car would take after it suddenly appeared made it possible for him to avoid a collision.

"On the night of February 21, 1961, I had a dream that actually came true—twenty-four hours later. I dreamed that my husband's brother had died and his wife called me long distance to tell me about it.

"In the dream she was crying and screaming, and I woke up terribly upset. I told my husband and, later in the day, a neighbor. They both just laughed at me, and said that dreaming of a death meant a birth.

"However, the next day we got the phone call. I answered. It was my sister-in-law, and she was crying and screaming just *exactly* as in the dream. She said her husband had been killed that morning. He had been topping a tree and fell.

"*It just can't be coincidence.* My husband has four brothers, so why should I dream about that particular one? It's so mystifying. I wish I knew what caused it."

A psychology teacher and his wife were sitting in their living room when they saw the shade of the table lamp slowly float upward for a moment and then slowly settle down again to its starting point. Within two minutes the phone rang; a relative was calling to say that the wife's grandfather had just died.

"Several years ago I [a woman from New York] had a business trip through the New England states. It was most essential that I have my dresses, which were in a medium-sized wardrobe trunk. I arrived at my destination, but the trunk did not. I had checked it in New York City and had my check. The men searched and traced but located no trunk. This went on until I would have had to return to New York City as I had only what I had on.

"Then in a dream I saw my trunk covered with snow on an isolated part of a station platform, and there was no check on it. I telephoned the man who was conducting the search and told him of the dream. Oh, did he scoff!

" 'Well, young woman,' he laughed, 'we don't find trunks by dreams.' I answered, 'You don't find them anyway. Suit yourself, and the company can put up about $1,000 in cash.' I found out that he phoned all along the route, found the snow-covered, ticketless trunk, and I got it with apologies. So this was not a case of suddenly remembering where I had left it."

One morning at breakfast a young Georgia schoolteacher dropped her fork and screamed that her fiancé, a merchant-marine engineer then on the high seas, was in danger. "He might be blown up any minute!" she shouted. She rushed to turn on the radio. A newscast was reporting that explosives had broken loose in the hold of a ship at sea and might go up at any moment. It was her fiancé's ship. The explosives were later secured, and the ship was saved. The teacher could not understand how she had been aware of the danger.

A woman in Pennsylvania dreamed that her four young sons had gone swimming, the nine-year-old wearing red trunks. "This was the only color that made an impression on me," the woman later recalled. As the dream progressed, the children were caught in an undertow. The mother jumped into the water and managed to pull out all but the one wearing the red trunks. Then she awoke.

Several weeks later her nine-year-old son was caught in an undertow and drowned. Although he owned three pairs of blue trunks, he was wearing a red pair of his brother's.

The eight experiences above are from the files of the Foundation for Research on the Nature of Man, established in 1962 at Durham, North Carolina, to continue the work of the Duke University Parapsychology Laboratory, which Joseph B. Rhine established in 1934. They are typical of the hundreds of thousands, possibly millions, of such occurrences that take place daily all over the world, in societies of all kinds, involving individuals of all types—the educated and the unlearned, the rich and the poor, the sophisticated and the naïve.

The adjective "psychic" is defined as "of or pertaining to the human soul or mind, mental (as opposed to physical)." In psychology the word pertains to "mental phenomena that cannot be explained otherwise than as originating outside of or independent of normal psychological processes." In relation to the subject of this book, the Random House Dictionary adds a fourth pertinent definition: "of, pertaining to, associated with, attributed to, or caused by some nonphysical force or agency: *psychic research*; *psychic phenomena*." The psychic world, then, is the world of the mind.

A psychic is therefore "a person who is especially sensitive to psychic influences or forces." After extrasensory perception (ESP) and psychokinesis (PK), the two subdivisions of parapsychology discussed in future chapters, had been brought into the limelight by the early researches at Duke University during the 1930s, an English psychologist, Dr. Robert H. Thouless, felt the need for a single label to apply to both of them. Dr. B. O. Wiesner, his collaborator, proposed the Greek letter *psi* because, like the algebraic *x* it was noncommittal. The process or processes by which psychic experiences are produced was thus characterized as an unknown. The suggestion was accepted, and since 1943 the term *psi* has been used in parapsychology whenever it is desirable to speak of the phenomena of the entire field. It is thus a more general term than either ESP or PK alone.

The word "phenomenon" (plural: "phenomena") is defined as "something that impresses the observer as extraordinary, a marvel." Certainly these adventures in the realm of the mind can, to say the least, be considered extraordinary.

What is psychic power and how does it operate in individuals possessed of it in one or another of its various forms? Psychic occurrences are not new. In ancient times—and even today in primitive societies—oracles, prophets, and soothsayers, using a practice called divination, foretold the future through omens and the interpretation of dreams. Necromancers conjured up the spirits of the dead for the purpose of magically revealing the future or influencing the course of events (sorcery). The mysteries of the mind were not unraveled for many centuries—indeed, they have yet to be fully explained—and superstition thrived. It is still prevalent even in our more enlightened times.

Twentieth-century research has investigated how individuals discover that they possess *psi* power and how it is used. It originates in the unconscious mind, and because it appears suddenly, that is, spontaneously, it may both appall and confuse the individual. Children are more apt than adults to have frequent psychic experiences. If they recount their impressions, however, they may be branded as different or strange, or they may be scolded for their "imaginings."

Susy Smith, a popular and prolific writer in the psychic field, expresses the effect of this discouragement on a child:

> Children who are branded as liars and dreamers when they tell of their psi experiences often feel misjudged and misunderstood for the rest of their lives. No child wishes to be set apart; he wants to be just like everyone else. He naturally develops a feeling of inferiority and insecurity when unjustly criticized and reprimanded. To be scolded constantly is disheartening as well as very confusing.

In writing about professional mediums and psychics, Miss Smith indicates that at least half of them exhibited their psychic gifts before they were ten years old!

> Those who did not become aware of them until they were older then realized the significance of certain childhood experiences of a psychic nature which they had not understood at the time. None of them as children had known they were different from others until it was pointed out to them because of what was considered their "peculiar" behavior.

Probably the most famous psychic in recent years was Eileen Garrett, who was president of the Parapsychology Foundation. Mrs. Garrett, who was active until her death in 1970 when she was in her late seventies, was considered to be the greatest medium of the twentieth century and one of the most important figures in the field. In her autobiography *Adventures in the Supernormal* she wrote:

> I have a gift, a capacity—a delusion if you will—which is called "psychic." I do not care what it may be called, for living with and utilizing the psychic capacity long ago insured me a variety of epithets, ranging from expressions almost of reverence, through doubt and pity, to open vituperation. In short, I have been called many things, from a charlatan to a miracle woman. I am, at least, neither of these.

Mrs. Garrett discovered her power when she was about four years old in Ireland. At that time she first saw "The Children," as she called them, two girls and a boy. They proved to be her daily and nightly companions until she was thirteen. They appeared to her at all hours, in the house and in the garden:

> We communicated freely, but without words. Sometimes they stayed for hours, sometimes only for a short time. Suddenly I would realize their presence, and as suddenly they would be gone. . . . When the time came for me to go to boarding school, I was fearful I might lose them, but they promised me that they would visit there.
>
> When I told my aunt about The Children in the early days of their coming, she ridiculed the idea of my playmates whom she had neither heard nor seen. . . . "But come and see them for yourself," I begged. "That will do now," she told me coldly. "I've no time to waste on your fancies. Just try to touch one of these children. You'll find there's nothing to touch."
>
> The Children laughed when I told them that my aunt did not believe that they existed. "We are wiser than she is," they confided. It was easy for me to believe this, for I knew that they did indeed exist and that my aunt was mistaken. However, I followed her suggestion and touched The Children. Their bodies were soft and warm. Yet they were different. I saw all bodies surrounded by a nimbus of light, but they were gauze-like. Light permeated their substance. When I once tried to explain this to my uncle, he said, "Yes? Well, maybe so," and I realized that even he did not understand.
>
> There came a time when I did not want to talk about The Children to anyone, but became cautious and secretive.

In later years, people suggested that The Children were fairies (a strong belief of the Irish), but when she first met them, Eileen knew nothing of fairies. People would also ask, "How did you communicate with them? Did you talk together?"

Eileen merely replied that they communicated by means of understanding each other. "No one ever understood," she maintained.

Another prominent psychic, Mrs. Ena Twigg, was the English medium whom Bishop James A. Pike first consulted in 1968, when he felt that his son, who had committed suicide, was trying to communicate with him. In an interview in the British periodical *Light* in 1965, Mrs. Twigg described her early *psi* experiences.

> I cannot remember a time when "things" were not happening with me, so they must have been doing so all my life. The earliest I remember was "going places." I seemed to be able to travel and see places hundreds or thousands of miles away. That faculty I now appear to have lost. . . . At 14 came my first tremendous experience. Going to bed one Monday night, I heard these spirit people talking. They said, "You're not going to have your daddy much longer. He will be with us by next Monday." My father was perfectly well, and it seemed ridiculous. I asked my mother what the "misty people" meant, and got scolded. On Friday my father slipped and fell, and by Monday he was dead. This made me very frightened of this strange faculty.

Mrs. Twigg finally accepted her abilities and later developed them with the assistance of a member of the College of Psychic Science, a British association for the study of psychical research, spiritualism, and related subjects.

The most famous teen-age psychic was Jeanne d'Arc (1412–1431). Her story is familiar, but it still seems incredible. A simple country peasant girl, daughter of a poor farmer, she nevertheless had visions and heard voices that told her she would lead the French armies in battle against the English, who had invaded and occupied much of France, and that she had only "a year and a little more" to accomplish her mission. It all happened just as the voices predicted.

Walter Prince, whose studies of psychic cases while president of the Boston Society for Psychical Research in 1924–1934 were published as *Noted Witnesses for Psychic Occurrences,* commented on this amazing clairvoyant experience.

> Were it not historical fact, but the invention of a fiction writer, it would all seem the wildest extravaganza. A peasant girl of sixteen, unable even to read or write, living in a village 200 miles from where the English were besieging Orleans and 400 miles from the court of the Dauphin, then kept from the throne by the English, the voices told her that she should go to his aid.

Jeanne was able to persuade six rough swashbucklers to accompany her to Chinon, where the French Army lay. She dressed herself as a man. After first being rebuffed, she persuaded the provincial governor to arrange an interview with the Dauphin. The Dauphin was skeptical, but her earnestness somehow impressed him. He had her examined by church authorities to be sure that she was not possessed, then made her head of the army.

Jeanne was able to dominate the hard-headed generals in a mysterious and unexpected way. She succeeded in lifting the siege of Orleans, drove the English along the Loire River, and finally defeated them at Patay in 1429 when she was seventeen years old. Her mission as outlined by the voices was accomplished when she stood beside the Dauphin at his coronation as Charles VII in the cathedral of Rheims and placed the royal crown upon his head.

Her reward proved to be tragic. Continuing her exploits, Jeanne was captured by the Burgundians, whose Duke was an ally of the British, and was later sold to the English, who were eager to destroy her influence over the people by putting her to death. The English turned her over to an inquisitorial court, which tried her for heresy and sorcery.

Jeanne's visions and voices proved to be her undoing. Threatened with torture, she made a retraction and was condemned to life imprisonment. When she later revoked her retraction, she was tried by another court and burned at the stake in 1431. Charles VII, the former Dauphin, made no attempt whatever to come to her aid during the trials, but he later recognized her services, and her sentence was posthumously annulled.

In a world where superstition abounded, Jeanne d'Arc was always under suspicion. The uncanny notion of visions was difficult to accept at the time. According to Andrew Lang, a Scots scholar of mythology and folklore, she was not an hysteric; the intensity of her belief was so great that she was able to convince the most suspicious and skeptical on even the highest levels.

Jeanne d'Arc's chief psychic ability was precognition (knowledge of the future), a type of extrasensory perception (ESP). For example, when she was en route to her first interview with the Dauphin, she entered a church and, after she left it, declared that the voices had told her to use a sword that would be found hidden under the altar. The sword was in fact found where she said it would be, and it is difficult to suppose that she already had information about it.

The prophecy of the voices that she "should last but one year or a little more" proved to be exact. In addition, on the fifth day of her trial, records establish, she asserted that "before seven years were gone, the English would lose a dearer engagement than Orleans," and that she knew it by revelation. This prediction was recorded in 1429, and the loss of Paris by the English in 1436 was its fulfillment. Of course, her two greatest predictions—raising the siege of Orleans and crowning the Dauphin at Rheims, both by her own efforts—were made at a time when they were least likely to come true, although both most certainly did.

At her second trial, when it seemed that her prison sentence would be upheld, she was asked in court whether her voices had promised that she should be liberated, and she answered, "Ask me in three months and I will tell you." She could not have then been told that her "liberation" would be by death, yet in retrospect, it seems as though the voices may have revealed it to her, for she was burned at the stake almost exactly three months after she made the prophecy.

Young people other than those who become professional psychics often have the *psi* ability but generally they do not follow up on it as Jeanne d'Arc did.

The limitations of distance do not exist for psychic

people. They can be aware of incidents taking place concurrently hundreds or thousands of miles away. Dr. Rhine has pointed out that anyone examining cases of *psi* soon became aware of the fact that space apparently loses its character, since the information was available regardless of where it was located, whether near or far from the person.

A concrete example, duplicated in various forms, is the Rhines' story of a young man working in a Wisconsin department store, four hundred miles from his mother and his former home. One day while he was busily waiting on a customer, he heard his mother call his name, loud and clear, and, to the amazement of his customer, he turned and answered, "Yes, Mother" in a loud voice.

Everyone who was standing nearby turned to him. He was very embarrassed and told the lady customer that he had distinctly heard his mother call.

He reported, "No need to say more except that I wrote my mother of my uncanny experience, and she wrote back that on that very day she was in the garden and wanted a hoe, and had momentarily forgotten I wasn't home and turned toward the house and called me, fully expecting an answer. Then she realized I was gone and felt funny about it all—but wasn't it strange that I heard and answered her four hundred miles away?"

The absence of the distance factor is very common. Another interesting example was reported by all the wire services and published later in newspapers throughout the country. It concerned an Army colonel from Michigan, who proved to be the last American to die in the Vietnam war, just eleven hours before the truce took effect on January 18, 1973. As an officer in the regular army, Lieutenant Colonel William Nolde of Mount Pleasant, Michigan, had fought in Vietnam since the early days of the war and his wife Joyce and their five children had not seen him for several years. He had written regularly, so that she at least knew that he had not been taken prisoner, though she did not know where he had been in action.

Before his death had been officially announced, Mrs. Nolde knew he wasn't coming back. "I knew it the other night. . . ." she reported. "I had a dream. A rocket came in and exploded." There was reason for some worry, for her husband had written that a captured North Vietnamese prisoner had told of a big push to come just before the expected truce. Mrs. Nolde said that in the dream "he said, 'Don't worry, honey, I'm all right,' and turned, and there was an explosion."

She told the children to be prepared because she had a feeling "Dad's gone." Within two days an Army officer came to the house to notify her that her husband had been killed at An Loc, sixty miles north of Saigon.

A friend on the spot later wrote her the details: "That night the town, a moonscape of rubble and dust after its long and successful battle against invading North Vietnamese, wasn't taking much fire. . . . Bill was just leaving the Ranger compound after saying goodnight to the province chief when the round came in." Taking into consideration the time difference, Mrs. Nolde's dream (a premonition or precognition) was fixed as occurring simultaneously with the event, the night before the ceasefire. Distance had not prevented her knowing.

This incident was much more than a mere coincidence.

The psychic powers possessed by certain individuals are not limited to a single type of experience. Extrasensory perception may take several forms. Through study and guidance, professional psychics may become skilled in many areas. An example is Edgar Cayce, who left well over fourteen thousand documented records of telepathic-clairvoyant statements he had given for more than eight thousand people over a period of forty-three years until his death in 1945. These "readings" are preserved by the Association for Research and Enlightenment, which he himself founded in Virginia Beach, Virginia.

Cayce, a simple, even rather unlearned man, was able in his trances to give detailed medical reports on people who came to him (and even on people who were far away) and to suggest cures for their illnesses. In addition to this medical "knowledge," he claimed, again in a trance state, to know what a subject's lives were in former incarnations, tracing them back through history and even prehistory to Atlantis itself, and made predictions of future events. Cayce and his sons, Hugh and Edgar Evans, published fifteen books dealing with various aspects of his work. Fourteen additional books have been written about him and his powers, while at least twelve others have sections devoted to his life and talents.

Cayce gave his first psychic reading in 1901 and the

last in 1944, so his comments on the development of psychic ability can certainly be considered valid:

> Unfortunately, we have all come to think of "psychic" as something very unusual, especially since the dictionary gives as one definition of psychic as "having abnormal powers." If we understood the real meaning of psychic forces, however, we would have a different conception as to the significance of developing such powers within ourselves. Whether we wish to acknowledge it or not, all of us have psychic forces. Whether we want to develop them or not is a different question.
>
> When people go about to develop any special ability or faculty, we know they go into training with that object in view [here he cites the conditioning of the body for a boxer, developing the voice, and the rules that must be followed in order to sing and play the violin or piano].
>
> When we develop our latent powers, we are working with something within which being is expressed. Our psychic forces give this expression. . . . We know that there is a definite faculty within our bodies and minds which we may call psychic forces or psychic power. We use the infinite mind, which is outside the realm of ordinary reasoning, and one must enter a state in which the finite [definite or definable limits] self no longer exists.

Cayce then goes on to describe how these inner knowledges of the mind are realized.

Several journalists writings for the general public on *psi* power, such as Hans Holzer, Sybil Leek, and Susy Smith, are unanimous in agreeing that one must be able to accept this gift and learn how to use it positively. Sources for tests are cited in an appendix.

Scientific researchers have investigated within the twentieth century the whys and wherefores of these powers, but the lay reader must be constantly aware of the many frauds and hoaxes that have been perpetrated on an innocent and unsuspecting public, causing a general feeling of disbelief and suspicion.

In addition, many people consider as psychic experiences events that are purely coincidental. For example, when the illness of a family member has been labeled terminal, a relative already has it fixed in his mind that death is certain and inevitable. The only unknown question is when it will take place. An involved person cannot help but think about the approaching end of a life. When he is told of the actual fact, it is all too easy for him to claim that he "knew" or "felt" it had come. We can suspect that this knowledge is psychic only if the time of death corresponds exactly with the time of the thought.

Knowledge of an event can be considered psychic only when it is immediately recorded and later checked, for memory can be tricky and confusing, with "experiences" taking on an element of fantasy and pure imagination, so much so that a person "remembers" something that he only imagined in the first place.

True psychic incidents, covered by the term "extrasensory perception" (see chapter 4), need to be distinguished from the popular concepts that are often confused or associated with them.

The development of parapsychology has been characterized by laboratory experimentation, the results of which have been continuously attacked by scientists. Scores of pseudo-scientific books and articles have been written on ESP, and lessons are even available on the "development" of psychic powers.

The general public rarely questions the validity of

many phases of the occult, accepting them as psychic. At a time when parapsychology is increasingly gaining respectability, the widespread antiscientific occult activity in the United States poses a threat to its recognition as a science.

The so-called occult sciences are extensions of long-accepted superstitions. They limit themselves mainly to forecasting through various nonmental means: astrology (foretelling the future by the stars); crystal-ball gazing (crystallomancy); tea-leaf reading (tasseography), palm reading (palmistry); and card reading (cartomancy), using either playing or tarot cards. Some of these practices are as old as mankind itself, but they are not substantiated by proof and are aptly termed by Herbert B. Greenhouse in *The Book of Psychic Knowledge* (1973) as "props" to bring on psychic experiences. According to Eileen Garrett, "Tea leaves, crystal balls, cards and the like probably serve as a form of concentration which allows the unconscious to reveal inner aspects of the mind."

In the author's *Superstition!* (1972), to which this book is related, he deals with the occult explosion, which reached its peak in the United States in 1969. At that time, fortune telling of all sorts had captured the interest of Americans in a manner that can aptly be termed phenomenal. In 1971, 10,000 professional and 175,000 part-time astrologers were reported to be active in the United States. Daily horoscopes appeared in 1,200 of America's 1,750 daily newspapers, with a total readership of 40 million. In 1969, an estimated 20 million Americans spent more than $150 million on personal horoscope material and $35 million on pamphlets and books. Psychologists aver that it was all due to the complexities of modern life and their effect on individuals.

CHAPTER 2

Psychic Power in Action

Before serious experimental study in the psychic area began in the 1930s, the principal attention of investigators had been paid to spiritualism, or the activities of mediums in supposed communication with the spirits of the dead. This included séances, table rapping, spirit photography, ghosts, and poltergeists (noisy spirits). Astral projection, reincarnation, and telepathy also attracted much attention in the nineteenth century.

Twentieth-century incidents of clairvoyance and precognition (foretelling the future) were received with both natural curiosity and outright disbelief. Persons gifted with such powers were thought to be "unusual," and something about them evoked a deep suspicion. Family members and acquaintances dismissed them as, to put it mildly, "odd," almost freakish. If an individual appeared to possess these powers, he or she frequently concealed the fact for fear of being misunderstood and even considered a mental case.

But with the coming of serious study of ESP in all its phases, belief in the existence of the psychic world became more respectable, and those possessing such powers were often envied. Beginning in the 1930s, interest in *psi* began to vie with the occult. The steady output of books written by investigators at Duke University brought the new science of parapsychology widespread national and international attention.

Books in Print lists over two hundred publications on various aspects of the subject in hardcover editions and almost three hundred in original and reprint paperbacks, most of them written by journalistic authors who are expert at making technical topics interesting to the general reader. The best-seller lists of the past decade have rarely been without a title dealing with some aspect of ESP. Whatever one might think of the phenomena these books describe, there can be no doubting that the interest they are responding to is itself nothing short of unprecedented.

Popular periodicals such as *Time, Newsweek, Life, Harper's, Ladies Home Journal, McCalls,* and *Mademoiselle* have considered the subject interesting to their readers. *Readers Digest* has published several chapters of selected books. Indeed, while the occult continues to interest millions, the psychic world is a runner-up that threatens to overcome its lead.

Why this interest? The subject is both new and intriguing. The human mind has always had a peculiar interest for us, and although in the past this appeal was mainly to students of psychology and human behavior, people in general are now suddenly realizing its vast complexity. These new revelations are closely related to their own experiences and to those of their kinfolk and friends.

Dr. J. Gaither Pratt, former assistant director of the Duke University Parapsychology Laboratory, and now at the University of Virginia, commented on this widespread interest in his volume describing the developments in ESP since 1960:

> Many times after I have given a talk about parapsychology, members of the audience have privately told me about their own psychical experiences. Almost always they say that they do not ordinarily talk about these things for fear people might think they are peculiar, or even crazy. But they are eager to share information with someone who obviously considers these matters important, who looks upon them as being quite normal, and whom they feel they can trust.

His book includes seventeen fascinating case studies showing the varieties of psychic incidents, and he has found all of them to be valid.

Psychic occurrences are not at all uncommon today. If readers of this book investigate and ask questions, they will be surprised to discover that they frequently happen among relatives, friends, or acquaintances. While the phenomena will vary, most of them will involve ESP.

The findings of the author while writing this book may be duplicated by the reader. Some of the following were already known by him; others were revealed on questioning.

Shortly after the Spanish-American War my mother's younger brother established himself in the Philippines as a United States manufacturers' representative. Thereafter my mother saw him only on his infrequent visits home. Nevertheless, she seemed to know many events of his life—his marriage, the birth of a son, a change in his business, and the like—before he wrote to her about them.

Her most unusual psychic experience involving him occurred during World War II. After the fall of Bataan, the International Red Cross notified her, as next of kin, that her brother and his wife had been interned in Manila by the occupying Japanese forces. She sent regular packages through that agency, but she always maintained—she was insistent on this—that, though they were received, they were never given to him.

When my aunt returned to the United States after the war, she said that the Japanese had not given them a single package, but that the soldiers had taunted the Americans by opening them in their presence. They could only view the soap, towels and washcloths, medicines, vitamins, shampoo, tooth brushes and pastes, and canned foods that were included, and desperately needed, before they were whisked away.

When General MacArthur launched his campaign to recapture the Philippines, my mother thought constantly of her brother and followed the progress of the Americans. When the newspapers reported that the United States forces were within one day of recapturing Manila, she was not at all exhilarated; she had "seen" him eating tufts of grass and "knew" that he was dead. My aunt corroborated this exactly later. Americans interned in Santo Tomas University had not been fed for a week because all the guards were assigned to the defense of the city; furthermore, the Americans had been reduced to eating the grass on the campus, with the result that my uncle died from the cumulative effects of malnutrition. He weighed a mere eighty pounds on that day so close to his release.

Two other family members received knowledge of deaths in identical occurrences many years apart. In the early days of aviation, my sister-in-law, then living in the Midwest, was flying to California where her father was seriously ill and at a crisis point. En route the prop plane was grounded in Texas after flying blind in a heavy fall of snow. She was resting in a hotel bedroom when the Venetian blinds began to rattle continuously. Not a breeze was stirring as the feathery snow fell outside, yet the shaking went on for several minutes. At the same time she strongly felt the presence of her father in the room (naturally she was thinking of him). With some difficulty she made telephone connection with her family, who told her that he had died; the exact time was when she had been setting her alarm clock before retiring. Was this a mere coincidence or a psychic experience?

More recently, my father, a clergyman, journeyed to England to act as summer minister to a congregation near London in an exchange agreement. Just before his departure from the United States, his sister-in-law in Texas notified him that his younger brother had been hospitalized, but that there was no reason for him to cancel his trip.

For two weeks before his first Sunday service in England my father traveled through the British Isles. When my uncle died unexpectedly, the family decided that he should not be told of his brother's death until he returned home.

Early one morning in a Scottish inn, my father was awakened by the continuous banging of the shutters, although there was no wind, not even a faint breeze. He fastened the shutter and thought no more about it.

The following Sunday was the first service of his summer pastorate in London. Afterward, he greeted members of the congregation at the main door. When he was finally alone, two women introduced themselves and said, "We appreciate the fact that your loss will evidently not affect your being with us this summer." Quite naturally puzzled, he asked them, why not, what loss were they referring to? One of the women showed him an obituary notice of his brother clipped from a Houston newspaper, and said relatives there had sent it to them, asking if their interim pastor was the Reverend Heaps who was listed as a survivor.

He kept the clipping and, recalling the incident in the hotel room, checked the date with his travel diary. On his return to the United States, he learned the exact hour of his brother's death and confirmed that the time difference coincided almost exactly with his Scottish experience. All this would not seem so unusual if he had known that his brother's condition had become critical—tales of feeling that a loved one has died are frequent when the individual knows of a serious illness—but that was not the case.

In almost every family one may find a person gifted

with ESP. In mine today, she is an in-law who maintains that this psychic power is sometimes frightening and "not to be played with." As a child, she saw her grandmother in a dream saying to her, "I'm dying, my dear child." She was awakened fifteen minutes later by movement in the halls and was told that a phone call had just been received with the sad news.

Most of her revelations come to her in flashes. "I may not have heard from or thought of the individual concerned for a long time," she says, "when I receive this very strong feeling about him or her . . . I *know* it is true. I always feel things about people I know and who have been close to me at one time or another.

"One time when my husband was facing a crisis in regard to financing his expanding business, I, like any wife, was very distraught. People he had trusted failed him, their promises made in supposed good faith had not been kept, and the bottom seemed to have fallen out. I could not get this worry and agitation out of my mind, and no amount of positive thinking seemed to calm me. One night when the situation had reached a decisive point, I felt the presence of my father, ten years dead; he walked in the door and I recognized him immediately because of his bald head."

Then she definitely heard him say, "You can go through anything. Pull yourself together, my dear. Everything is going to work out all right." Within two days the situation was solved in both the financial and personal aspects. Did he appear to her because she was psychic and attuned to him, or was the incident merely a figment of her imagination.?

This same relative also predicted the earthquakes

that devastated Southern California, where she lives, in February, 1971.

A woman friend in Connecticut told me about many incidents of precognition and clairvoyance involving her family and friends throughout a decade. "Scores of times," she declared, "I have had rather uncanny mind experiences when I have felt strong warnings of danger, almost always seeing the persons involved. Within hours these have proved to have happened concurrently." Three such episodes, as recounted in her own words, are indicative of the way in which such psychic endowments operate.

"In many suburban areas, friends and neighbors having swimming pools share them with other families lacking them. These are generally scheduled on warm summer days. One day I dropped off my young son to enjoy a swim. I was to call for him after I had completed shopping and a number of errands. Within an hour, while in a supermarket, I felt that he was in danger. I even saw him on the bottom of the pool at the deep end. So strong was this feeling that I left the market immediately without completing my shopping, giving a tip to an attendant to replace the items I had already selected on the proper shelves.

"The pool was about half a mile away and I broke the speed laws and even ran through stop lights in getting there. I rushed to poolside, and failed to see my son either in the water or near it. The children told me thay had not seen him for some time, and I circled the pool to the deep end. He was lying on the bottom! Two of the older boys dived in and brought him out. He was not breathing and had turned purple. Fortunately, one of the boys had learned resuscitation procedures as a Boy Scout. Meanwhile the hostess had telephoned the police for an ambulance and oxygen. Before its arrival, after what seemed an interminable time, Jimmy was finally revived. Had I not received this 'message,' he would not have been noticed and would definitely have drowned.

"At another time, I wanted certain rooms in my home to be painted, and employed an old man who had previously worked for a local firm. He was available on a free-lance basis and, since time was no object, I told him to work only when he felt like it, to stop when and if he became fatigued. When he arrived one morning, he appeared to be tired and his progress was more than ordinarily slow. Before I left the house, he assured me that he would rest and leave for the day if he felt unwell. He had covered a part of a wall at the time. After I had been absent about an hour, I had this familiar feeling that something was wrong at home. In a fleeting mind picture, I saw him lying on the drop cloth next to the upset ladder. I rushed home, and there he was as I had seen him. The doctor later told me that his fatal heart attack had occurred at approximately the same time that I had become aware of it.

"After we moved to California, I continued to see and feel events as they happened, often at long distances from where I was. For example, my son, then a college student, was driving home for Christmas from the northern part of the state. He had telephoned just before he started out, so quite naturally I was thinking about him and hoping that he was not forgetting the speed limit because his car, to my way of thinking, had too much power for its size. I was almost paralyzed when I saw his car leaving the concrete highway, skidding on the gravel and turning over into a ravine. The picture was frighteningly vivid, and I waited for word of the accident, which I received by telephone from the hospital to which he had been taken. Fortunately, he was not dead, but had suffered a severe head concussion when he was thrown against the windshield.

"You ask what my feeling is concerning this 'gift.' Well, it is hard to live with because I never see happy events; they are always serious. A psychic friend once suggested that, perhaps without realizing it, I *will* the misfortunes which I foresee. But that is not at all true. I am not what might be called a worrier. They just happen."

Individuals possessing *psi* powers are often disturbed by the revelations they receive. When these revelations involve people they don't know or situations in which they are not personally involved, they are faced with the predicament of whether or not to make the knowledge known, often to complete strangers, although it might be valuable and useful if accepted by them as valid. Two of the author's friends in Connecticut were faced with this dilemma during the writing of this book in mid-1973.

In a nearby town, a seven-year-old Brownie left her home late one afternoon on her bicycle to deliver some girl-scout cookies to purchasers and to pick up a butterfly she had hidden under a rock two days before. When she failed to return home by dinner time, her parents followed the road in the direction she had gone and found her abandoned bicycle. A search of the nearby wooded areas before darkness proved futile, and she was thought to have wandered into the thick underbrush and become confused and lost.

Neighbors organized an all-night search, and early the next morning hundreds of volunteers under the direction of the Connecticut State Police set out on an exhaustive, hill-by-hill hunt on foot, horseback, and motorcycle. Later, a helicopter summoned from the Army National Guard flew so low that it brushed the treetops.

Returning horseback riders reported that the underbrush was so thick that a seven-year-old child could probably not make her way over the area. One of them remarked that "a kid will take the path of least resistance, and I don't see how she could travel for any length of time through such undergrowth," leading to later acceptance of the belief that she might not have wandered off at all, but had been kidnapped. Continued searches over an ever-widening area proved ineffective. The child had completely vanished, and flyers with a picture and a detailed physical description of her and of the clothes she was wearing at the time of her disappearance were distributed throughout the state.

On my return two months later, my psychic friends told me about strong feelings that had arisen in them about the child. These feelings had come to them individually as vivid pictures. One had "seen" an abandoned automobile on a small ledge parallel to the road; the road was a gravel one, not a paved highway, and the car was a faded blue. The girl's body was in the trunk. The other friend had "seen" in a dream a similar automobile abandoned in a gully; its color was also a rusty blue, and she "knew" the girl's body was to be found in the trunk.

These pictures had appeared to each of my friends separately, and when they compared them, they considered going to the state police. As they said to me, however, "You know what the reaction would be. They would dismiss us as foolish and crazy."

I agreed to accompany them on an automobile tour of the area previously covered by the searchers. For almost three hours we systematically traveled over the unpaved country roads. Not only did we see almost two dozen abandoned cars both near the roads and in the distant undergrowth, but many were of a faded blue color! Was this a coincidence? we asked ourselves.

Each time an automobile was sighted, I went over to it and tried to raise the trunk, though after this period of time, the sense of smell would have located a decomposing body, if one were inside. Some of the cars were in gullies, others near a road, a few parallel to it. A few were almost hidden in thick underbrush and overgrowth.

The search proved futile. At the same time, because the body had not been found, the state police finally called in the FBI, as is usual in kidnap cases.

Meanwhile, one of my two friends met another woman socially, and they talked about the unsolved disappearance of the child. My friend spoke of her vision, and the woman said, "My God, that's exactly what a friend of mine who was visiting me at the time wrote later to me! After she returned home, several hundred miles away, she was thinking (not dreaming) about it one night and saw a faded blue automobile and knew the decomposed body was in the trunk!"

The same pictures came to these individuals independently. One can only wonder when or whether their identical *psi* experiences will eventually be corroborated. As of this writing, eight months after the incident, the case has not been solved.

Psychic experiences are far more common that one would ordinarily suppose, and evidence indicates that a large number of persons who have such experiences accept them without question. A Gallup poll was devoted to this question a few years ago, and 10 percent of those asked admitted having had one or more experiences that convinced them that ESP occurs. Other surveys agree on the 10 percent figure.

According to J. Gaither Pratt:

> From this, we can conservatively estimate that more than one hundred million persons now living have learned about ESP at firsthand. This estimate is probably far too low. Not only is it below ten percent of all living adults, but it also fails to take account of children who have had psychic experiences.

A 1967 survey of 2,500 eight-grade boys and girls, aged eleven to thirteen, made in Uttar Pradesh state, India, revealed that nine hundred (or 36 percent) reported certified ESP experiences, additional evidence that children are more psychic than adults.

The most controversial figure currently riding the crest of the popularity of parapsychology is Uri Geller, a twenty-five-year-old Israeli who has in a very short time become an international celebrity for his demonstrations of the four types of ESP—precognition, clairvoyance, telepathy, and psychokinesis (moving objects without touching them). One of his standard performances of the latter is bending spoons and keys apparently by the force of his thoughts. In late 1973, he claimed to have demonstrated his powers more than 1,400 times since he arrived on the psychic scene four years before.

Geller says he first discovered he was clairvoyant at age three. "My mother would come home from playing cards and I would tell her how much she had won or lost, exactly."

His powers of psychokinesis manifested themselves when he was seven. "I was sitting one day in school looking at my wristwatch," he told an interviewer, "and I noticed the hands were jumping ahead to a different hour. Then, later, when I looked at it, I could see that the hands were bending. At first I didn't connect any of this to myself. But then I realized I could do things other people could not do."

Geller explains that his powers are "one power divided into three or four." When he uses telepathy and clairvoyance, he says, he actually visualizes what he is receiving "on a kind of television screen in my mind."

Psychokinesis occurs when he tells himself over and over what he wants the object to do. All these manifestations, he maintains, require the presence of friendly and receptive people. In fact, according to *Time* magazine, he failed to demonstrate his powers on a Johnny Carson program because he felt that Carson was hostile. (This explanation for failure is common among all *psi* performers, especially mediums, when tested under controlled conditions.) He claims to have learned to leave his body and journey to distant places, and admits to be practicing mediumship in communicating with the dead. His object, he says, is "to master all the psychic disciplines."

As a matter of course, the authenticity of his feats has been widely challenged: Is Geller a true psychic or a magician? On the latter point, magician Milbourne Christopher, who specializes in the exposure of psychic charlatans, has called him "nothing more than a trickster who can be exposed by people skilled in deception." Christopher claims that any good magician can duplicate Geller's feats.

Others are equally critical. *Time* magazine's Israeli correspondent reported that Geller came under suspicion when a group of psychologists and computer experts from Hebrew University duplicated all of his feats and called him a fraud. Eventually, he left the country in disgrace. The majority of his critics feel that if all his demonstrations were genuine, he would be "the wonder of the psychic world, since he would have mastered all the *psi* areas as well as the borderland practices."

To offset the growing controversy, Geller spent five

weeks during the last months of 1973 at the Stanford Research Institute, one of America's largest and best-known think tanks. This investigation was its first in the psychic field. Under intense scrutiny and control, Geller ran through the gamut of his abilities:

- He predicted the throw of dice all eight times he tried (precognition).
- He guessed, twelve times without error, which one of ten aluminum cans contained objects (clairvoyance).
- He transmitted to the institute's vice-president a number the latter was thinking of (telepathy).
- He bent a laboratory balance under a bell jar without touching it (psychokinesis).

In their report, the two physicists who conducted the tests rendered no decision regarding Geller's psychic powers, stating only, "We have observed certain phenomena for which we have no explanation."

But again there was disagreement and controversy. A professional magician, James Randi, known as "The Amazing Randi," had been present during the tests. He duplicated each of Geller's feats, explaining that any professional magician could perform them. In rebuttal, the institute insisted that its researchers had not been duped. "Whether the subject be a saint or a sinner," commented a spokesman, "has nothing to do with our measurements concerning the so-called awareness of individuals."

At the time of this writing, Geller has agreed to be retested in order to maintain his credibility. However, the fact remains that Geller, with his expert showmanship, introduced the range of psychic powers to millions of ordinary citizens who formerly were either unaware of them or suspicious of such performances.

Among entertainers in nightclubs and on television in the field currently, the most prominent is without question George Kreskin, who is billed with only his last name, generally as the Amazing Kreskin. However, though his feats cover all types of ESP, particularly telepathy, Kreskin does not consider himself to be a psychic, maintaining that his mental feats "are probably hypersensitive or hypernormal rather than extrasensitive. In the manner of a concert pianist who has spent much of this life at the keyboard, my mental communication has been developed through years of painstaking practice." In his autobiography, *The Amazing World of Kreskin* (1973), he rejects the idea that ESP, as popularized by Dr. Rhine and the parapsychologists, is "a contradiction, suggesting that we have the ability to perceive beyond our senses. Really, how is that possible?" And he asks facetiously, "Perhaps we should just expand our range of senses, blindly, to seven or eight? Who's to know that eighteen or twenty-two don't exist?"

Though Kreskin admits to producing effects that might be attached to the somewhat questionable "psychic senses" area, he confesses:

> I don't understand many of them. Obviously something happens to me and suddenly I'm talking about a subject that I should not, in the conscious awareness, know. At the same time, I don't believe this is "psychic," as we commonly accept

> the word. Likely, the awareness is triggered because of my trained sensibility.

Yet, in public performances, his feats indicate that he possesses *psi* power, and he reluctantly admits picking up information through

> a kind of telepathy. . . . By deep concentration, "tuning in," I seek out and then "receive" a single thought, provided that the sender is concentrating to an almost equal depth . . . . The best I can do in answering questions is to say that the *perceived thought,* traveling invisibly, arrives in the same form as any other thought. I accept the perceived thought; it is suddenly there, and I act upon it, without any particular evaluation. However, I firmly believe that public demonstrations of thought perception should not be considered as absolute proof of the scientific possibilities of ESP. Demonstrations such as mine should be considered as examples of the particular skills of the performer.

Kreskin covers his powers with the inclusive term "suggestibility." He apparently uses no tricks, though he performs the usual feats of illusionists, usually with cards or sealed envelopes, to gain audience interest and a rapport with his audience, what is called in the language of the stage "warming up an audience."

As yet, he has not been "exposed," and has not been a subject of controversy, for his feats appear to be authentic. How else, one may ask, can telepathic feats such as the following be accomplished?

• Kreskin concentrates on the contents of a woman's purse or a man's wallet, asking them to think of the number on their Social Security cards, and visualizes it almost immediately.

• He telephones well-known persons, such as Carol Burnett, asking them to concentrate on an object in the room where they are. Without any clues, he describes the object in detail.

• Using twenty-two telephone directories of cities throughout the country, Kreskin chooses a name and number from one of them, writing this information on a piece of paper which he places in a sealed envelope and gives to the television host or nightclub master of ceremonies. He asks a member of the audience to choose any directory among them; meanwhile he "orders" the subject to select, for instance, Dallas, Texas. The subject invariably chooses the correct phone book, and is given a copy. Holding his copy of the book over one arm, Kreskin begins thumbing through the pages until the individual says, "Stop." He then directs the subject to close his eyes and select a name by running his fingertip over both the pages. Kreskin pinpoints the name by mental suggestion, and if the connection is made, the name will prove to be identical with that in the sealed envelope. Only rarely does he fail.

Kreskin is assuredly a mentalist, and an effective one. That his many accomplishments are due to psychic power cannot be denied; whether they are truly due to ESP, which he maintains they are not, remains an unanswered question.

Another in-the-news adventurer into the *psi* world is ex-astronaut Edgar Mitchell, who while on the 1971 Apollo 14 moon mission conducted telepathy experiments with four friends on earth who claimed to have psychic abilities.

During his free time he sent ESP test symbols to be

received by them. The plan was intended to be kept secret until the results could be fully analyzed and announced at a later date, but one of the receivers could not resist the temptation to announce his participation during the space mission.

This breach of confidentiality forced Captain Mitchell to seek the aid of professional parapsychologists in analyzing his results and making a report on them immediately. When this report appeared, there were some indications that ESP had successfully spanned the distance between the earth and the space ship, since fifty-one out of two hundred messages reached his receivers on earth. But according to Dr. J. Gaither Pratt, the success achieved was not outstanding as compared with many other ESP experiments:

> On a conservative basis of evaluation, about one time in twenty the total score made on the experiment would have been expected by chance—and the question of the relation of ESP to distance was certainly not fully and finally answered. But a new trail was blazed and this is enough to have accomplished on this first exploration of ESP as a possible means of communication on a universal scale. Indeed, it requires no great stretch of the imagination to think that Apollo 14 will be remembered as the historic occasion on which the first ESP test in outer space was made.

After his retirement from the Navy, Mitchell set up the Institute for Noetic Sciences, a foundation for investigating psychic phenomena (noetic means "of or pertaining to the mind") in Palo Alto, California. "The overriding concept is that all psychic concepts seem to be under the control of mind," he stated at the time, "and that by properly understanding mind, or consciousness, and its functions we will come closer to understanding the nature of man." His investigations thus far have covered all types of ESP, as well as psychic healing.

Mitchell's foundation helped to finance the Geller experiments at the Stanford Research Institute, and he has enlisted seventy-six educators, psychiatrists, scientists, and businessmen to serve on the board of advisers. A book edited by Mitchell titled *Psychic Exploration, A Challenge for Science* (1974) includes chapters on all phases of parapsychology written by specialists.

Newspaper editors appear to consider anything regarding *psi* experiences as highly interesting to their readers, and the wire services regularly send out to their subscribers stories that would have been rejected only a few years ago. One such account appeared while this chapter was being written. It involved psychometry, the linking of people and events with a particular object by means of ESP. Another name for it is object reading, and it is a form of clairvoyance. An object is given to a psychic for the purpose of stimulating him to draw from its contact information associated either with its history or with the history of the person to whom it belongs or once belonged. The object may give information (and did in this case) about a locality rather than a person.

In the reported case, the two young daughters of Mrs. Joanne Tomchik of Burnt Hills, New York, aged three and five, had disappeared with their divorced father on his visiting day in April, 1972. Since then Mrs. Tomchik had spent $6,000 on private detectives in a fruitless search for the girls. Last summer she heard a radio program on parapsychology and "as a last resort" got in touch with the program's originator, the Association of Parapsychologic Study and Investigations, a private group in nearby Saratoga Springs. The group referred her to their "most gifted" member, Mrs. Millie Coutant, a fifty-five-year-old bookkeeper, to whom she sent pictures of the children. For an entire afternoon Mrs. Coutant studied the photographs intently.

"I just kept looking at the lines in the pictures," Mrs. Coutant said, "but it was really my first try at psychometry." On a tape recording she told Mrs. Tomchik of her "vision" of a trailer and a light-blue truck with Carolina license plates; she was unable to determine whether they were South or North Carolina.

Mrs. Tomchik wrote to authorities in both North and South Carolina with the information and gave them a description of her former husband, Andrew. He was found a month later, living with the two girls in a trailer in Wilson County, North Carolina. The light-blue pickup truck, with North Carolina plates, was found parked nearby.

In an extradition hearing, Tomchik was accused of violating his visiting permit, and the girls were returned to their mother.

Mrs. Coutant had begun to think seriously about her psychic powers only six months before all this happened. She took some tests and, as she put it, "From then on, I just kept on being right about predictions; and when you're right all the time, you begin to get confidence."

The case is even more interesting because she was comparatively inexperienced. However, the talent existed in her mind and needed only her concentrated attention to produce results.

One of the most fascinating current uses of *psi* power is in crime detection. Though generally suspicious of clues produced mentally, police who have become hopelessly baffled are increasingly enlisting the assistance of psychics.

Their revelations often include a full physical description of a murderer and information about his habits and background (valuable in identifying him), and about the place where he might be found. They often furnish complete details about the murder itself: the setting, the method, the weapon, and the appearance and actions of the killer and his victim. Sometimes photographs of the suspects, if any, are shown to a psychic in the hope that one can be identified. The police follow up these clues in locating the murderer.

Information gained through so-called psychic powers is not admissible as legal evidence in court, so a psychic detective is valuable only in finding the offender. Any court case has to be based on what is actually found.

For a number of years the limelight in psychic crime detection has been focused on Peter Hurkos, a Dutchman, who has become world-famous. According to Norma Lee Browning, his biographer and a professional journalist-skeptic, writing in *The Psychic World of Peter Hurkos* (1970), Hurkos fell from the fourth floor of a building in The Hague while working as a painter when he was thirty years old. In addition to a broken shoulder, he suffered a brain concussion, and when he regained consciousness, he endured severe headaches "like knives in the head." He soon began displaying a newfound power. He told his doctors and nurses about things that had happened to them in the past, and predicted future events.

Hurkos has been using the "vibrations" he began receiving then for the last thirty years or so. His career as a psychic detective began in 1950, when he located the British Coronation Stone after it had been stolen from Westminster Abbey. Through mental impressions and pictures, he identified the thieves as prankish students and finally told where the stone could be found—the ruins of an ancient abbey in Scotland.

Though apprehended, the students were not arrested, the affair being publicly characterized as "a harmless escapade." Scotland Yard insisted that Hurkos had nothing to do with finding the Stone, even if he did actually point out its hiding place. Because his assistance had been underrated and he had received neither recognition nor monetary award—one had been offered but not paid—Hurkos left England and spent the next five years in Paris, working with the French police, again with little or no publicity.

Time and again thereafter his assistance went officially unrecognized by authorities even though they had depended on his powers. Furthermore, when something went wrong, he was invariably criticized and his work belittled. The smallest inaccuracy on his part became the signal for unmerited denunciation as a fraud.

Hurkos was never able to overcome the distrust of

those with whom he worked. "It was almost as if they did not want to recognize the aid I was giving them," he says.

An American neurologist, Dr. Andrija Puharich, who had established a foundation for experiments in mind phenomena—ESP, telepathy, and hallucinations—heard of the by-now-famous Dutchman, and brought him to America. This doctor was the same one who would sponsor Uri Geller when he left Israel a decade later.

Hurkos then began his career as a crime consultant and psychic detective. Working with the Miami Police Department in 1958, he helped solve a double murder committed on the same day. He also told the authorities that missing Florida judge Curtis Chillingworth and his wife had been abducted and their bodies tossed in the ocean. They had been put in a rowboat, he said, then beaten with oars and dumped overboard to the sharks. Their bodies have never been found, but he accurately described their murderer, who was later apprehended, tried, and sentenced.

The next year he was summoned to assist in solving the murder of a Virginia family, husband and wife and two small daughters, after the authorities had 165 suspects, an unusual number, under investigation. Though Hurkos said the murderer could be found locally, the FBI discovered him in another state. That was because the suspect Hurkos identified had moved, and Hurkos had therefore spotted the wrong man at the address he had received psychically.

The most famous criminal case in which Hurkos was

involved was that of the Boston Strangler in 1964. Hurkos was called in after the eleventh in a series of ghastly murders, when public pressure over the failure of the Boston police to make any progress in solving them was intense. Massachusetts Attorney General (later senator) Edward Brooke had taken over the investigation.

Hurkos worked five days, describing in detail each of the stranglings and pinpointing them accurately on maps. For the eleventh and most recent murder, he described the killer and told where he could be found, and the man was finally located.

This man, never named publicly, and Albert De Salvo were the principal suspects. Though Hurkos had picked the other man, De Salvo confessed (in detail), was tried and sentenced to a state institution for the criminally insane. The suspect identified by Hurkos was committed to another mental institution, and the psychic still insists that Albert De Salvo was *not* the Strangler.

After being discredited in the Boston Strangler case, Hurkos was involved in three other events. The first was the mysterious disappearance in 1967 of American Jim Thompson, a prominent silk merchant in Thailand. Hurkos unreservedly maintained that Thompson was kidnapped and taken in a truck to Cambodia. However, because the man he named as being behind the kidnapping was the Prime Minister of Thailand, Hurkos was not allowed to enter that country to follow up on the clues he had received. The case has never been solved.

In 1969 Hurkos helped investigate the murders of

two coeds at the University of Michigan and at Eastern Michigan University, which are a few miles apart. The murders were not related, however. The University of Michigan murderer was apprehended and tried; the other was not.

Hurkos also gave information leading to the arrest of Charles Manson and his cult members in the 1970 mass murder of seven persons at the Hollywood home of Sharon Tate, a film star.

Hurkos has admitted to Jess Stearn, author of *Adventures into the Psychic,* that he is not infallible, but his record of 80 percent accuracy has as yet not been matched. He looks equally into the past, present, and future, producing visualizations that are acted upon by the police. In these probings he reveals facts that might not otherwise come to light—a formidable and almost frightening power.

Human experiences and happenings that are known to be psychic exert a tremendous appeal, and they awaken interest in all who learn about them. On the one hand, the average layman, though strangely puzzled, feels a sense of awe at these evidences of the mental world, and since he lacks any knowledge that might help him to analyze the phenomena, he will probably not question their validity. On the other hand, those who possess a scientific and analytic turn of mind tend to doubt seriously the authenticity of such experiences. Such persons may comment, "They are certainly very interesting and colorful. But did they really happen? What about the possibility that the experience and the information revealed through it was only a figment of the imagination, that it never actually took place?"

In spite of their other world character, however, psychic phenomena will continue to have an increasing claim on the attention of serious investigators.

CHAPTER 3

The New Field of Parapsychology

From ancient times through the Middle Ages until the beginnings of science, all mental experiences have been linked with superstition because they defied explanation on any human level. Life was regulated by signs received from the gods or from unearthly, mysterious, and therefore mystic sources.

The Old Testament is filled with what can now be recognized as accounts of psychic experiences, and the prophets used clairvoyance and precognition in their guidance of the Israelite nation. Dreams, whether they foreboded ill or predicted reassuring, far-reaching changes, were recognized as a means for seeing into the future.

In *The Book of Psychic Knowledge* (1973), Herbert Greenhouse has compared the Biblical prophets with modern psychics in these words: "They had psychic experiences during altered states of consciousness. They had visions and dreamed dreams. They heard voices. They went into trance, induced by music and in a measure by the mystery of the desert through which they often traveled."

These experiences continued in the New Testament. For example, the apostle Paul recounts his visions and dreams. Jesus, of course, particularly in his miracle healings, proved to be the outstanding psychic in the Bible; in addition, scores of his prophecies came true.

The Greeks and Romans relied upon oracles for advice to govern their actions. The priests and priestesses revealing the oracles accompanied their revelations with ritual, and great reliance was placed on signs and omens. Prophecy was definitely related to magic. The powers of the oracles supposedly came from the gods and goddesses, and no important undertaking was planned without consulting Delphi or some other prophetic shrine. In Rome the most noted oracles were the ten female sibyls, whose predictions for the future of the empire had been collected in a series of books, to which a special body of priests referred in times of national emergency.

The Dark and Middle Ages were the periods in Western European history that followed ancient times. Mysticism flourished, and saintly men and women often had visions, which were considered visitations from God.

With the advent of modern history and the development of the sciences and the increase in education, people began to question any experience that seemed out of this world. By the late seventeenth and early eighteenth centuries they were beginning to have doubts about accounts of supernatural activities.

During the nineteenth century in England, however, spiritualism enjoyed enormous popularity. The activities of mediums were widely publicized and séances, table rapping, levitation, automatic spirit writing, and spirit photography were all the rage. Many of the stately ancestral homes suddenly and inexplicably became haunted by ghosts.

The vogue for spiritualism was taken up by all social classes, with the poor embracing it as devotedly as the aristocracy, among whom séances had become fashionable. Nevertheless, few of the mediumistic exhibitions were genuine. For every authentic medium, like D. D. Home, there were scores of charlatans and amateurs.

The first scientific investigations in England were undertaken between 1873 and 1880 by a group under the direction of Henry Sidgwick, professor of philosophy at Cambridge University, and his wife Eleanor. Working with highly respected and honorable mediums, they established that spiritualism, though based on religion, might be considered a psychic practice.

This and other inquiries led to more organized research through the formation of the Society for Psychical Research in 1882, with Sidgwick as president. The vice-president was Alfred Balfour, who was later to become Prime Minister of England and president of the organization in 1893. He had discovered that he possessed clairvoyant ability.

The aim of the society was "to approach the problems presented by alleged phenomena scientifically and without prejudice or prepossession [advance opinions] of any kind." The objectives were "an examination of the nature and extent of any influence which may be exerted by one mind upon another, hypnotism, clairvoyance, inquiry into apparitions and haunted houses, and spiritualism." The results of its investigations were to be published in its *Journal.*

The society, the oldest of such organizations, is still active today. It has validated or disproved literally thousands of cases of psychic power other than spiritualism: clairvoyance, precognition, telepathy, and the like. Emphasis was focused on ESP and its branches when research on the subject came to the fore in the United States during the 1930s. When the society receives reports of ESP experiences, it thoroughly investigates them, and its negative conclusions have often resulted in heated acrimonious controversy.

Spiritualism dates from 1848, when two young girls of Hydesville, New York, Margaret and Kate Fox, achieved national attention by their "spirit rappings." Although the Fox sisters were exposed as frauds, many mediums made their appearance through the years, and the most reliable traveled regularly to England.

Others were not as fortunate. The 1870s and 1880s was a period when several famous mediums were exposed as charlatans, and because of it, the American Society for Psychical Research was established in Boston in 1885. It became a branch of the English organization in 1887, and independent again in 1905. Like its counterpart, it continues to be active, having turned its attention to other psychic areas during the early years of the present century.

Despite the frauds, interest in spiritualism grew, reaching a peak during and after World War I. In 1920,

William McDougall, a well-known British psychologist, was appointed head of the Psychology Department at Harvard University. At that time he was also president of the British Society for Psychical Research, having become interested in the subject while a student at Cambridge University. He discovered that his predecessor at Harvard had exposed the great Italian medium Eusapia Palladino and that an experiment in telepathy had been carried out by one of the professors in the department. McDougall obtained funds for further research by department members. Their main achievement was the investigation of "Margery," a Boston medium.

While at Harvard, McDougall was contacted by a young Chicago botanist, Joseph Rhine. Rhine and his wife Louisa had become interested in psychical research, partly because they had heard a lecture on spiritualism given by the English physician Sir Arthur Conan Doyle, who was also author of the Sherlock Holmes stories. Rhine began correspondence with McDougall, and in 1926 he joined the Harvard Psychology Department as a research assistant.

McDougall felt that psychical research should be given attention as a university course of study, and at a symposium at Clark University he presented the pros and cons of the question. Such research, he stated, could render a service by "giving final answers to problems which mankind has long answered with ready-made formulae, handed down from the dim dawn of human reflection, and before which it now halts with burning desire for certainty or unsatisfied longing for more light." The points he made covered the problems encountered later by the Rhines at Duke University.

When McDougall joined the Duke faculty in 1927, Rhine went with him, and together they established the Parapsychology Laboratory.

The term "parapsychology" was introduced by Dr. Rhine to replace the older English term "psychical research." It is defined as "the study and investigation of phenomena that are not explainable by known natural laws." Such occurrences are described as "paranormal."

Parapsychology, then, is the study of psychic abilities. Parapsychologists prefer the Greek letter *psi* to the popular word "psychic," but the two terms have the same meaning.

It must be emphasized again that parapsychology does *not* deal in general with astrology, magic, palmistry, fortune telling, witchcraft, or any other occult practices. The psychic abilities that are covered in this relatively new branch of study can now be clearly described. They are those that enable a person to make contact with the world around him without the aid of his senses or muscles. Parapsychology deals entirely with mental phenomena.

The main divisions of parapsychology are derived from the two broad types of observed phenomena with which it deals: extrasensory perception (ESP) and psychokinesis (PK). These two main types of *psi* interaction make up almost the entire field covered by parapsychology thus far. The general types of ESP phenomena are telepathy, clairvoyance, and precognition. Investigation into other psychic fields began in the 1960s and will be discussed in the last chapter of this book.

When he established the Parapsychology Laboratory, Dr. Rhine and his staff formulated ground rules for investigation. The reliability of reports on spontaneous (nonlaboratory) personal experiences had to be authenticated. Experimental methods were introduced, and tests in all phases had to be devised. This was truly a pioneer operation and its techniques have of necessity been continuously improved and perfected through the years. They cover all divisions of parapsychology.

Rhine's great task of bringing order to the study of psychic phenomena has been successful in making ESP a respectable subject. Prior to the Duke studies, many scientists still regarded psychic investigation as foolish nonsense, and when Rhine published his early results, they immediately attacked his methods. Many are still suspicious and skeptical.

The main reason for such criticism, parapsychologists maintain, is that, since *psi* is an unknown, nonphysical force, established scientific methods cannot fit its investigation. Therefore many scientists contend that parapsychologists are not engaged in scientific research at all.

Professional clairvoyants and mediums—the technical name for them is "sensitives"—have not proved to be effective when involved in *psi* tests, and not many have been willing to participate. Dr. Rhine believes "they are probably afraid the tests would be too severe for them." On the surface their exploits seem immensely impressive, but too often they are dramatic rather than scientific. (Uri Geller and Peter Hurkos, discussed elsewhere, are examples.)

Daniel Cohen, a well-known writer on ESP, offers suggestions as to why this situation exists:

> Is the elusiveness of some professional sensitives, due to the prima donna qualities of a great artist and performer? Is it because the cold laboratory setting destroys their delicate abilities? Or is it a deliberate evasion to avoid exposure as a fraud? You can take your pick of the reasons.

Scientists operate under definite sets of rules and investigative procedures which in most cases are long established. The mysteries with which parapsychology deals were—and are—completely new in that they cannot be explained in terms of accepted scientific laws. Since ordinary testing techniques could not be applied to the facets of ESP, entirely new methods had to be devised. Since these research techniques were unfamiliar, scientists tended to judge them on the basis of their own patterns to which, quite naturally, they did not conform. The scientific method appeared not to have been followed.

Attacks began with the publication in 1934 of Dr. Rhine's book *Extra-Sensory Perception*, in which he revealed the results of his early research on ESP with Duke University students. He became the target of a great deal of criticism, particularly from psychologists. Much of it was ill-founded and some highly abusive, and considerable emotionalism was evident among his supporters as well as his detractors.

The principal criticism was that Rhine's statistical calculations were invalid. He was dismissed as a dedicated missionary rather than a dispassionate scientist weighing facts impersonally. Commenting on the ESP tests, H. L. Mencken, the unsparing critic of all things American at the time, wrote, "In plain language, Professor Rhine segregates all those persons who, in guessing the cards, enjoy noteworthy runs of luck as proof that they must possess mysterious powers."

Dr. Rhine responded to these challenges by improving and perfecting his testing techniques, and further confirmed the existence of ESP in *New Frontiers of the Mind* (1937) and *The Reach of the Mind* (1947).

The disagreement and hostility of scientists erupted again during the 1950s, with a seemingly endless barrage of criticism. The position of scientists was summed up bluntly, with no holds barred, in a 1955 article in *Science* magazine by Dr. George R. Price, a British chemist then at the University of Minnesota, titled "Science and the Supernatural." Dr. Price contended that proof of ESP was conclusive only if one were to accept the good faith and sanity of the experimenters, but that it could easily be explained away if one were to assume that the experimenters, working in collaboration with their witnesses, had intentionally faked the results.

After examining in detail many of the principal tests, Dr. Price, in conclusion, made the following observation: "My opinion concerning parapsychologists is that many of their conclusions are based on clerical and statistical errors, so that the results are dependent on deliberate fraud or mildly abnormal mental conditions." Since *Science* was the official organ of the influential American Association for the Advancement of Science, this critique reached an extensive specialized audience.

(Dr. Price's article admittedly made parapsychology suspect, but in a complete reversal seventeen years later, early in 1972, he apologized in *Science* for his attack on Dr. Rhine, writing, "During the past year I have had some correspondence with J. B. Rhine which has convinced me that I was highly unfair to him in what I said in my 1955 article.")

Rebuttals by the leading parapsychologists at Duke and elsewhere were printed in subsequent issues and the controvery was discussed in general news magazines as well. Bergen Evans, who was expert in debunking false beliefs and superstitions at the time, wrote one of the most devastating criticisms of parapsychologists in an essay titled "Psiing in the Carolinas," ending it with this statement: "Their claims are so contrary to the view of the world worked out with painstaking care by scientists over the past 300 years that to accept them would mean rejecting almost everything upon which modern thought depends." Perhaps without realizing it, Dr. Evans had put his finger on the crux of the controversy.

The most active opponent of parapsychology during the past decade has been Professor C. E. M. Hansel of the University of Wales. He visited Duke University in 1959 to investigate some of its experiments and wrote two separate criticisms, which were published in the *Journal of Parapsychology* along with replies from the experimenters under attack.

For a while Hansel's criticisms appeared to have been

effectively answered, and he was silent. Then, in 1966, he published a popular book entitled *ESP: A Scientific Evaluation*, in which he attacked the entire field of parapsychology. He not only repeated his previously published criticisms against such investigations, he also widened the scope of his attack. He took apart in detail all the major experiments in both the United States and England, the result being his opinion that *all psi* research past and present was "a form of cheating, trickery, deceit, conspiracy, and a complete fraud."

Dr. Hansel's criticisms were so scathing and all-inclusive that readers of his book who were not already well informed about parapsychology tended to accept them without question, and temporary damage resulted. But, wrote Dr. J. Gaither Pratt later, "parapsychology will survive Hansel's disruptive efforts just as a great city survives a riot."

George Kreskin, currently one of the most prominent psychic performers, has characterized Hansel's critique in these words: "In the name of science, a remarkably biased debunking of all parapsychological research." His opinion is shared by many professionals.

The attitude of scientists to the "fringe science" (note the limiting adjective) of parapsychology has changed steadily decade by decade. Two polls of six hundred members of the American Psychological Association made in 1938 and 1952 showed that the attitude of psychologists toward the study of ESP had become significantly more favorable in spite of the current attacks.

Using the same multiple-choice questionnaire late in 1972, the editors of *New Scientist*, an English scientific magazine, received 1,500 replies from readers, most of them scientists. Twenty-five percent of the respondents believed ESP to be "an established fact," with a further 42 percent declaring it to be a "likely possibility." Only 19 percent believed ESP to be a "remote possibility," while 12 percent considered it merely an unknown, with 3 percent considering it an impossibility.

To determine the acceptance of parapsychology, the question "Do you consider the investigation of extrasensory perception a legitimate scientific undertaking?" was included. A huge 88 percent replied "yes," and 20 percent answered that the study should be regarded as a form of psychology. More than half, however, considered that parapsychology was making "little, if any, progress." Since the majority of respondents were working scientists and technologists, these opinions on such a controversial topic cannot be lightly dismissed. As the editors commented, "Clearly, a large number of serious scientists consider it to be highly interesting and potentially immensely significant branch of science. At the same time it is fair to comment that the ranks of those who support parapsychology appear to be sharply critical of the slow progress it is making." The final comment pinpointed the crux of the continuing problem: "In sum, it seems that cool, fresh winds may be needed to blow prejudices away on both sides."

As noted above, the focal point of criticisms by scientists has been centered around the use of ESP tests constructed and perfected by the Duke experimenters. Speaking of these tests, Dr. Hansel wrote, "Experiments testing for the presence of extrasensory perception are fortunately of such a nature that anyone of reasonable intelligence can understand them and even try them out for himself. Many persons are put off at the start, however, because they have a false impression of the amount of evidence that has accumulated." In examining the various card-guessing and dice-throwing experiments repeated over hundreds of thousands of experimental runs with thousands of different persons, he concluded that, in this opinion, many of the tests had been rigged to obtain the desired results. "It is necessary to discuss openly possible trickery or cheating by participants to produce a spurious conclusion," he stated specifically. "If the result could have arisen through a trick, the experiment must be considered unsatisfactory proof of ESP, whether or not it is finally decided that such a trick was in fact used." He thereupon set forth his own idea of the standards that should be applied. Dr. Price, and the many other scientists who were critical of Dr. Rhine's work, also pointed out the possibility that error and trickery had been used extensively. But at each attack Dr. Rhine and his Duke associates were apparently successful in overcoming these criticisms.

The field of parapsychology has had more than its share of frauds, charlatans, and opportunists. But even those critics who were openly skeptical about the phenomena reported by Dr. Rhine and his staff seldom questioned Rhine's personal integrity. But in the late summer of 1974 Rhine was forced for the first time to acknowledge publicly a scandal that, according to *The New York Times*, "periled psychic research just as parapsychology seemed to be making solid headway toward scientific acceptability."

This crisis involved the falsifying of experimental data by Dr. Walter J. Levy, Jr., the director of the Institute for Parapsychology This subterfuge was discovered by Dr. Levy's own associates.

Until that time, the work of Dr. Levy, considered a protégé of Dr. Rhine, was regarded as among the most impressive of the reputable attempts to show that psychic phenomena exist. Levy's research was aimed at testing the ability of rats to anticipate events (ESP) or to effect physical changes by sheer will power (psychokinesis). He continually reported a success of 50–55 percent, which was very high.

One of his assistants became suspicious when he noticed that Dr.Levy appeared to be needlessly tampering with the recorder, causing his tape to score high. Three associates secretly watched many experiments. A set of identical instruments, installed without Dr. Levy's knowledge, confirmed their suspicions by recording a much lower score. The director resigned after admitting that he had falsified experimental data to force the results he desired.

Fakery is nothing new among scientists, however. A few months before the Levy deception was discovered, the public learned that Dr. William Summerlin, a researcher at the Sloan-Kettering Cancer Center, had been painting experimental mice to make it appear as if a new procedure for cancer had worked. Before the Levy exposure, Dr. Rhine had published an article in The *Journal of Parapsychology*, "Security Verus Deception in Parapsychology," in which he conceded that the honesty of ESP investigators had long come under suspicion. Indeed this suspicion is one reason for the long delay in acceptance of parapsychology as a reputable science. He suggested that "this subtle, slightly distasteful, and sometimes embarrassing issue of fraud might need more frank and forthright recognition and response." He even noted that "apparatus can sometimes be used as a screen to conceal the trickery it was intended to prevent." He also outlined the precautions that have to be taken to "insure the product of any scientific field against errors of observation, recording, logic, evaluation, reporting and other uncertainties," and indicated safety measures which could be applied to prevent experimental deception.

After the Levy incident had been thoroughly investigated, Dr. Rhine officially discussed the case in another article, "A New Case of Experimenter Unreliability." Though, for "humane" reasons, he called Dr. Levy "Dr. W," readers, because of the widespread publicity, readily identified the offender. When he'd written his March article, he said, "I had not expected to come back to the subject in print. I thought experimental parapsychology was heading into a successful avoidance of problems of experimenter dishonesty. Accordingly, I was shocked to discover, only a few months later, a clear example of this problem at the Institute, involving an able and respected colleague and trusted friend."

Dr. Rhine again referred to the Sloan-Kettering incident, contending that if the field of immunology could have a Summerlin incident without marring the reputation of the field as a whole, parapsychology should be able to do the same. Nonetheless, he said that the Levy episode provided incentive for researchers to design experiments less susceptible to fraud, which he said was far more common in all fields than was usually believed. "The idea of putting faith in the personal honesty of a research worker is old-fashioned," Dr. Rhine said.

For the present, however, this much-publicized incident may be considered a major, if temporary setback in psychic investigation. Leaders in the field and skeptical critics agree that, since for many years parapsychologists have worked hard to purge the field of the trickery and the biased experiments that were once common, the Levy affair will have considerable impact.

Dr. Rhine looks upon parapsychology as an already established young science. He compares it to the state of the physical sciences in the eighteenth century when scientists were aware of natural forces like electricity or magnetism but not really able to understand them.

The profession of parapsychology has developed amazingly in recent years. In August, 1965, Dr. Rhine, the grand old man of parapsychology, retired and ended his nearly forty-year association with Duke University. He then became director of the Foundation for Research on the Nature of Man in Durham. There the Institute for Parapsychology has continued the work of the Duke Laboratory, with its facilities and records transferred. Financial support has been made available principally by the late Chester F. Carlson, the inventor of xerography, who left 2 percent of his estate, or a million dollars, for psychical research.

Dr. J. Gaither Pratt, Rhine's former assistant, now teaches at the University of Virginia in the Division of Parapsychology headed by Dr. Ian Stevenson, whose specialty is telepathy. The division has established a dream laboratory to investigate ESP.

The development of parapsychology has led to the formation of two new professional and research organizations. The Parapsychology Foundation, established in New York City in 1951 by the late Mrs. Eileen Garrett, has as its purpose the support of research into all facets of ESP and paranormal phenomena. The foundation publishes a series of monographs and the *Parapsychology Review.*

The Parapsychological Association was founded in 1957. It became affiliated with the American Association for the Advancement of Science in 1969. The vote for this action by the latter's 135,000 members, scientists and engineers, was a landmark step in the recognition of parapsychology's validity, and one of the most encouraging signs of changing public and scientific attitudes toward psychical research. The association publishes *Proceedings*, which covers reports from many countries on a wide range of topics.

Parapsychology has now become a recognized study in colleges and universities, mainly because young people are intensely interested in it. The "occult explosion" in the 1960s attracted many of them to witchcraft, ghost stories, and the like, and became a national phenomenon. Part of the interest arose at that time from the college generation's involvement in psychedelic drugs and meditation. More recently, in their continued pessimism and anxiety, they have turned to parapsychology in great numbers.

According to a 1971 article in *Mademoiselle* magazine:

> The current groundswell may be viewed as a rejection of traditional sciences and the uses to which they have been put. After all, science has failed to solve the pollution problem and it certainly has done nothing to advance the cause of world peace. How can you look to science as any kind of guide when there are so many issues on which scientists cannot agree—like the SST (supersonic transport plane), birth control pills, marijuana, drug rehabilitation, even Vitamin C and the common cold. . . . Still others maintain that this youthful interest is not rebellion against science, but a drive to develop it further, by treating parapsychology as one of the new frontiers of knowledge. For whatever reasons, the interest *is* strong.

In spite of opposition, in some cases from members of the psychology and science departments, courses in parapsychology were being offered in more than a hundred institutions in 1973. The University of Michigan and Duke University offer credit for independent study of the field, and graduate study is increasing. Young people are becoming volunteer summer interns in various research centers throughout the country, and extension courses are attracting an ever-increasing number of adults.

Sources of information on parapsychology study are included in the appendix.

Scientists in other countries tend to hold the same views on ESP as those in the United States. Only a few laboratories are located in overseas universities, and most research is undertaken by scattered individuals and organizations.

However, scientists and psychologists in the Soviet Union and its satellite countries began investigating parapsychology intensively during the 1960s. This activity has developed so amazingly that the resulting situation has been aptly compared to the earlier U. S. S. R.–U. S. race in space technology, a contest in which Russia at first outdistanced the United States.

While competitive to a degree, the Soviet research appears to be geared to extending the areas developed in America for proving the existence of ESP and PK. The Russian parapsychologists harbor no doubts about the existence of parapsychological phenomena. Instead, they are seeking practical applications of them, especially in medicine and health. The leading American researchers realize that cooperation will prove mutually beneficial in probing this "enigma of the unknown."

In the summer of 1971 Dr. Stanley Krippner, director of the Dream Laboratory of Maimonides Medical Center in Brooklyn, and a research assistant visited Russia. A report in *Saturday Review* afterward revealed hitherto unknown aspects of the U. S. S. R. activities. Like the United States, the Soviets have established six major centers for parapsychological research and about a dozen minor ones, all government-funded.

Dr. Edward Naumov, director of the Institute of Technical Parapsychology in Moscow and the leading figure in that country, was astounded when told of the ever-present problem of funding research in the United States. Indeed, he was incredulous. "Don't your people realize the importance of parapsychology in the development of the human mind?" he asked. "This is extremely important work that you are doing, for it opens the door to creativity and human potential. Your country is a nation of businessmen. Don't they realize it is good business to support humanistic efforts?"

Proudly Dr. Naumov produced a list of the names of forty-five parapsychologists whose work was being subsidized, balancing it with nine names who were critical of such research.

The differences in definitions of parapsychology reveal the Soviet emphasis on biology rather than on the mind. Though the Russians are using many American investigative techniques, they are also charting new courses, and the veil of former secrecy is being lifted, to the benefit of research.

Even so, visits by Americans and the resulting exchanges of information are greeted with official suspicion. In the spring of 1974, for example, Dr. Naumov was sentenced to two years at hard labor for refusing to break his contacts with his Western colleagues. The charges were said to have been fabricated after Naumov ignored secret police demands that he cease meeting with foreign specialists visiting Moscow.

Recognizing the Russian advances, many Americans feel that the American government should sponsor and give financial support to such research. This has not as yet been done except in a few special projects undertaken by the Air Force and the Department of Health, Education, and Welfare.

Late in November, 1971, Representative Claude Pepper of Florida requested that an article by one of his constituents be inserted in the *Congressional Record.* It was a proposal for the establishment of a task force for metapsychiatry (a new term for parapsychology and one that is more inclusive) to meet the Russian challenge. Dr. Stanley Dean, a Miami psychiatrist, expressed the Soviet "threat" in these words:

> Having pioneered in the exploration of outer cosmic space, the Russians seem determined to pioneer the penetration of inner psychic space as well. . . . The late Leonid Vasiliev, first chief of the state-funded laboratory for parapsychology at the University of Leningrad, stated uncompromisingly, "The discovery of the energy underlying ESP will be equivalent to the discovery of atomic energy." It seems to me that our country can no longer be indifferent to such a challenge.

Though the practice of inserting speeches and articles on a wide variety of subjects into the *Congressional Record* is common, such items are only meant to be informational. Unfortunately no congressional action will be taken on Dr. Dean's recommendation.

In backing his proposal, Dr. Dean cited a highly praised and controversial 1970 book, *Psychic Discoveries Behind the Iron Curtain*, by Sheila Ostrander and Lynn Schroeder. It should be considered "must" reading for anyone interested in these developments and their relation to the work of American parapsychologists. The authors cover all aspects of the subject in Russia, Bulgaria, and Czechoslovakia. Dr. Rhine called it "a bold, stupendous job of lively reporting, complete to the most fantastic fringes." *Psychic* magazine hailed it as "not only a fascinating book but a potential bombshell. . . . This book may do for ESP what Sputnik did for space travel."

The future directions in which psychic research will move are almost unbounded. As studies of ESP and related phenomena are extended, the disclosures will assist in unraveling the mysteries of the mind.

CHAPTER 4

Facets of Extrasensory Perception

Through the years the testing techniques at the Parapsychology Laboratory conformed to precisely defined research conditions, and thousands of subjects have been used. A "subject" is a person who is experimented on. He or she is also called a "percipient," or "receiver." The person who administers a test is termed the "agent" or "sender," and it is his mental state that is to be conveyed to the percipient. This relationship is crucial in all testing.

The first work at Duke covered both clairvoyance and telepathy, but the former soon took precedence. The clairvoyance tests at Duke during the 1930s were of very simple design and have undergone little change since.

The identification of concealed cards proved to be the best method of testing, and a simplified card deck, larger than ordinary playing cards, was devised. The deck consisted of twenty-five cards, five each of the following symbols printed in heavy black ink: a star, a rectangle, a cross, a circle, and wavy lines. Slight modifications were made in these symbols from time to time.

Eventually the deck became known as Zener cards, after Dr. Karl Zener, the staff member who invented them. They have been published and can be purchased from sources listed in the appendix.

The procedure used is very simple. After the subject has been shown the deck and told the nature of the test, the deck is shuffled and placed face down on the table at which he is seated. The experimenter sits opposite, with recording materals, a sort of score card or call record. The subject is asked to try to identify the top card, and when he has made his "call" by naming one of the symbols, his answer is recorded and the card is removed without being looked at. The next card is called, recorded, and removed, and so on until the deck is finished.

The cards in the deck are then checked against the call record to discover the number of successes or hits (correct answers). The deck is again shuffled and cut and another run (calling of the deck) is made in similar fashion.

From chance alone the average score expected was—and still is—five hits per twenty-five cards. The total number of hits, or deviation, above this chance expectancy of five is the final score representing the subject's ESP power.

Adam J. Linzmayer, an undergraduate psychology student at Duke, who proved to be the best performer in the early tests, went through the deck of cards over seven hundred times during the first three years of work. This man averaged about eight hits per run of twenty-five trials, better than three hits above the expectation for each deck. By ruling out the element of chance,

Linzmayer's performance was so astounding that it proved to be a landmark in ESP investigation at the time. The average for other high-scoring individuals proved to be seven hits per twenty-five cards. However, the standard finally became sixty hits in a series of three hundred guesses. This was attributed to the fact, later established, that the highest scores in ESP experiments are generally made early in a series of trials and gradually decline, not because of fatigue but because of the attitudes of the subjects toward the experiments. This is termed the negative factor or decline effect.

The role of chance or coincidence has always been an important factor in evaluating ESP tests. If this were not done, the scores would be open to misinterpretation. Coincidence is, of course, common in ESP esperiences, particularly those concerning clairvoyance and precognition of death.

As Arthur Koestler points out in *The Roots of Coincidence* (1972).

> The non-mathematician seems to have a more acute awareness than the specialist of the basic paradox of the probability theory [a theory in which a specific value indicates the chance or odds that a given event will occur] over which philosophers have puzzled ever since Blaise Pascal initiated that branch of science for the purpose of improving the gambling prospects of a friend. The paradox consists, loosely speaking, in the fact that probability theory is able to predict with uncanny precision the overall outcome of processes made up out of a large number of individual happenings, each of which in itself is predictable. In other words, we observe in ESP tests a large number of uncertainties producing a certainty, a large number of chance events creating a total outcome.

Koestler is troubled by the fact that since probability operates successfully in mathematics, physics, genetics, and even economics (business relies on it), ESP experimenters are forced to conclude that some factor other than chance is involved. "We are driven to it, but we are not happy about it," he asserts. "If card-guessing were all there is to parapsychology, it would hardly be worth bothering about it." For that reason, experimenters are still seeking to explain this ever-present factor.

When published in 1934, the results of the first ESP tests caused an anticipated controversy. But the seed had been sown, and testing began at many other institutions. The highest published scores recorded outside of Duke were those of a twenty-six-year-old woman tested by Professor Bernard F. Reiss of Hunter College, New York City, in 1936. In seventy-four runs of twenty-five guesses each, she scored one with all correct, two with twenty-four, and an average of 18.24, this against the established score of five.

The highest consistent performer in tests to detect the power of ESP has been Pavel Stepanek, a Czech who became a star in the 1960s and is known in parapyschological circles as "P. S." While working at the information desk of the city library in Prague, he came to the attenton of Dr. Milan Ryzl, a chemist who had turned to parapsychology and who claimed to be effective in training ordinary persons to demonstrate ESP through hypnosis. Ryzl tested Stepanek's powers, with spectacular success.

On a trip to Europe in 1962, Dr. J. Gaither Pratt of

Duke visited Prague and met both the mentor and his subject. They worked with cards with one side white and the other colored, concealed in opaque covers. As each of these covers was held horizontally in front of him, Stepanek simply guessed whether the colored or white side of the hidden card was turned up. Pratt worked with the young Czech without using hypnotism only three days, the period of his visa. On a second visit he continued the tests. Eighteen months after the first visit, Pratt returned again to Prague with two colleagues, an American and and a Dutchman, as observers.

Meanwhile, the Czech experiments of Ryzl had attracted international attention, and the usual controversy had arisen over their validity. Observers arrived from several European countries, and three Dutch scientists, after working with Stepanek alone as well as in the presence of Ryzl, finally determined that the same results could be achieved with or without hypnosis. The vital relationship between the experimenter and the subject could therefore be established ordinarily as at Duke and other centers.

In 1967 Dr. Pratt returned to Prague for additional testing, with Dr. J. G. Blom, a researcher from the University of Amsterdam. Dr. Ryzl did not participate in those tests. This time the cards were sealed in envelopes before being hidden inside the covers. Four thousand guesses were recorded in four lengthy sessions, and Stepanek scored a total of 2,154 hits. Although this was only 154 more than the 50 percent level expected by chance, it nevertheless was high enough to rule out happenstance or mere luck as a reasonable explanation. It proved to be a record in the field.

Stepanek has visited the University of Virginia three times since then, and Dr. Pratt has maintained correctly that Stepanek "has produced in his ESP results a new and unexpected effect. [This refers to his naming the colors of hidden cards with results that were 100 octillion times better than chance.] . . . The search for what it means, for the new light it may throw upon the nature of ESP, has kept investigators working steadily with the feeling that they may be near to making a breakthrough in the research. . . . The account of Stepanek's accomplishments may seem like a serialized novel that is interrupted at the most exciting point with the tantalizing phrase 'to be continued.' "

The urge to conduct scientific investigations into unchartered territory must come from the research workers themselves. As Dr. Pratt states it, "Scientists working on the frontiers of research are like explorers of the earth who have felt compelled to turn their dreams of discovery into the reality of journeys into remote and unexplored places."

Though card-guessing experiments have been the principal tests for ESP because of their simplicity, the main objection to them has been that the constant repetition involved leads to understandable boredom and fatigue in both the experimenter and the subject, the decline effect previously mentioned.

For a short period, therefore, the Duke Laboratory experimented with the reproduction of drawings, but that method was soon discontinued because the results were difficult to assess.

Telepathy and precognition have also been under examination at Duke and elsewhere. In telepathy, the subject is separated from the experimenter by a screen that is placed on the table between them. The experimenter then thinks of a card symbol that might be transferred to the subject. Because this form of thought transference is very difficult in an experimental situation, only the most receptive subjects respond. Mind reading is still somewhat puzzling to researchers.

A classification of the Duke collection of cases of precognition, made in 1954, revealed that 40 percent of the ESP cases reported had to do with future happenings.

The role of dreams in ESP phenomena is a comparatively recent development in parapsychology. New knowledge of dreams has opened the way for researchers to determine the emotional background of such experiences. According to Sigmund Freud, a subconscious part of the brain is just as alert during sleep as it is during waking hours and accepts any image, which it presents in great vividness to the dreamer. Thus dreams often seem larger than life, more convincing and brilliant, and even more real than life.

Before parapsychology was established, the Society for Psychical Research (London) conducted many experiments on the role of dreams. When ESP experiences began to be evaluated, it was imperative that this phase be scientifically studied.

Parapsychologists have special reasons to be interested in dreams. Collections and accounts of ESP experiences from daily life show that the majority of these experiences occur as dreams. This fact suggests that the dream state may be especially favorable for the expression of ESP abilities. Recent studies connected with what happens in sleep have revealed the course of sleeping and dreaming; that is, scientists can tell when the sleeper begins to dream, how long the dream lasts, and when it ends. They have also discovered that if a sleeper is awakened as soon as a dream has ended he is almost always able to remember what it was about.

Dream laboratories are a comparatively new development. The most active and productive in relation to parapsychological research is in operation at the Maimonides Medical Center in Brooklyn, New York, which was established in 1964. According to Dr. Stanley Krippner, its director, in five of every eight experiments conducted since, there has been "a statistically significant" exhibition of phenomena hard to explain by any yardstick other than mental telepathy.

Many of the studies are based on the use of famous paintings, a method developed by Dr. Montague Ullman, head of the hospital's Psychiatry Department. In one such study, an agent sits in a room in another building and attempts to convey his thoughts about a certain objective painting to a subject sleeping in the soundproof room in the Dream Laboratory. The sleeper is hooked up to an electroencephalograph, which records his brain patterns on graph paper. When the machine shows that the sleeper is dreaming the experimenter wakes him up over the intercom and asks him to describe his dream, and his words are tape-recorded. Later the dreams are compared with the painting for evidence of ESP.

The subjects' accounts of their dreams have fitted the target painting with amazing accuracy. Since chance in ESP accounts for only 50 percent hits, scores such as 64 or 91 percent, for example, are dramatic. Other experiments at Maimonides have involved clairvoyance and precognition, again with valid positive results.

Other centers are also investigating dreams. The Menninger Foundation has set up a laboratory in Topeka, Kansas, and a Sleep and Dream Laboratory is now in operation at the University of Virginia.

The question of whether drugs play a part in bringing about *psi* experiences has been the subject of much study. Many young people who take drugs become involved in the occult and, to a lesser extent, the psychic world. In *Your Mysterious Powers of ESP*, Harold Sherman explains this trend:

> Instead of making a sustained conscious effort for self-development to activate the higher powers of mind, young people are seeking mind expansion and greater sensual pleasures by the shortcut methods of hypnotic, electrical, and chemical devices. Their fragmentary experiences with hallucinations, fantasies, distorted visions, and dreams have aroused curiosity and caused them to believe that if these illusory sensations could be explored, perhaps more could be learned about the mystery of life, including the mystery of their own selves. Young people, new to the field of sensation, willing to try anything once—and more often than that if they discover there are thrills and kicks in it—are more prone to the mental and emotional adventures that give promise of spiritual illumination.

> Unhappily, what has resulted thus far has been, in the main, more confusion, bewilderment, demoralization, frustration, fears, insecurity, and despair of finding the ultimate reality or any dependable reality at all.

The attitudes of most parapsychologists is that the *psi* function that may seem to be released through drugs is invalid and ineffectual. The Duke experimenters determined that in tests for both ESP and psychokinesis (PK) the effect of narcotic drugs, when used in heavy dosage, has been to interfere with positive scoring and to produce "chance" results that are completely unreliable. The same is true with alcohol.

Therefore, instead of revealing true *psi* ability, drugs retard its discovery. A drug user only imagines that he possesses psychic power.

Do animals possess ESP powers? The Duke parapsychologists have answered with a guarded "yes." Experiments with cats, dogs, and horses in the 1950s indicated that their behavior is often influenced by *psi* power. A complication, however, is that clever animals, generally dogs or horses, can be taught to respond to verbal questioning (or hand signals) by tapping or pawing the correct number of times, or selecting by nose or mouth lettered blocks from a tray to spell out words and sentences. Such tricks have always been part of animal acts on the stage.

The most tightly controlled study on a "clever" animal was that done on Chris, the Wonder Dog, owned by George Wood. Chris came to the attention of the Duke parapsychology researchers through his ability to respond to verbal questions by pawing the correct number of times on Mr. Wood's forearm. The Duke worker suggested that Wood teach Chris to guess which of the five standard ESP symbols were enclosed in opaque envelopes, by pawing once for circle, two for cross, and so on. Chris learned to go down through a stack of twenty-five such cards, guessing their identity with a high degree of accuracy, even though no one else, not even his master, was present. His guesses were recorded by a machine, and when all guesses were completed, the results were checked. However, when the Duke researcher was present as an observer, Chris's performance dipped far below chance; this was the "negative factor" or "decline effect" previously discussed.

Dr. Rhine's tests with a three-year-old horse, Lady, of Richmond, Virginia, for a six-day period in the late 1950's, gained national attention. Her owner, Mrs. Claudia Fonda, had trained Lady to work with letters and numbers, and the filly would respond to both spoken and silent commands to spell words or make computations by touching her nose to the appropriate symbols printed on blocks. Rhine wrote on pieces of paper questions which could be answered by a number or a single word. He would show the question to Mrs. Fonda, who would ask the horse to tap the number or spell out the word she was thinking of. Precautions were taken so Mrs. Fonda wouldn't give clues visually or through her voice. First she turned her back when asking questions. Later a screen was placed between them, and finally Rhine replaced Mrs. Fonda in asking the questions. Yet Lady continued to make high scores.

Whether or not animals possess *psi* abilities has not yet been adequately proved. Obtaining uncued responses under laboratory conditions is at best difficult. Too often, the so-called ESP response is not genuine; resulting instead from previous training. At present, the best evidence involves consideration of natural instinct.

More convincing are the performances of domesticated animals who find their way home over long distances, sometimes after having been taken away in closed vehicles by an indirect route. Examples of animals traveling many hundreds of miles have been reported and such reports involve many different species.

Even more baffling are the incidents, fewer in number but still numerous enough to be impressive, in which a pet animal—dog, cat, or bird—left behind when its human companion departed for a new location, escaped later and followed him. After some weeks or months such animals arrive at the new destination, sometimes hundreds of miles away, where it has never been before.

Those unfamiliar with ESP maintain that such travels are due to instinct and smell, sight, and sound, but there is a growing belief that these animals are psychic.

Bird, fish, and animal migrations, generally an annual occurrence, are still puzzling, too, particularly where direction is concerned. In *The Hidden Springs* (1973), Renée Haynes comments on this phenomenon of nature:

> Numerous experiments have been carried out in the hope of discovering something about this faculty of direction finding.

> They have achieved little more than the establishment of the fact that it can be exercised in other circumstances than those of migration. . . . Experiments indicate that . . . starlings, swallows, storks, terns and petrels removed from their nests, taken in various different directions and released, flew straight home over distances of up to a thousand miles, and they flew the shortest way home.

Regarding both animal and bird migrations, Miss Haynes claims that some form of paranormal cognition is involved in animal direction finding.

Additional research will be necessary, however, before we can comprehend these phenomena.

CHAPTER 5

Telepathy

Simply defined, telepathy means "sending or receiving messages without using any of the five senses (hearing, sight, smell, taste, and touch)." It is commonly referred to as "thought transference," that is, the ability to know what another person is thinking. Since the advent of parapsychology, however, it has come to be known as "direct awareness of the mental state of another person."

Interest in telepathy developed from the personal experiences in thought transference that have been reported as common occurrences in every land and throughout recorded history. In such cases two people, such as close friends or relatives, might have the same dream on the same night, or they might try to get into contact with each other, simultaneously, by telephone or mail, with some common thought or purpose in mind that could not have been conveyed by the senses.

During the heyday of interest in telepathy in England, during the late nineteenth and early twentieth century, numerous experiments were conducted. These investigations were linked with the great interest of the

British in spiritualism and thought transference through mediums.

However, one of the most productive students of telepathy was a nonprofessional. Professor Gilbert Murray of Oxford University, a world-famous classical scholar, revealed during his presidential address to the British Society for Psychical Research in 1915 that he had achieved considerable success in telepathic experiences which he had undertaken with members of his family. His procedure was very simple and uncomplicated.

> I go out of the parlor and of course out of earshot of my family and friends there. Someone in the room, generally my eldest daughter Rosalind, thinks of a scene or an incident or anything she likes, and says it aloud. It is written down and I am called into the room. I come in, usually take my daughter's hand, and then, if I have luck, describe in detail what she has thought of. However, the least disturbance of our customary method—change of time, the presence of strangers, and especially noise of any kind—is apt to make things go wrong.

The subject of Murray's informal experiments, which he continued until 1929, ranged from incidents in the lives of those taking part to scenes from history and fiction, as well as imaginary events thought up especially for the situation. Hundreds of these telepathic incidents were investigated and reported on by at least two reliable psychics who were members of the British Society. They ruled out the possibility that Murray could have heard the discussions of his companions when they were selecting a subject to be used in a particular test, and concluded that they were genuinely telepathic.

Out of the first five hundred tests studied, a third were judged successful, while 30 percent were rated as partially successful. The remaining 40 percent were failures. Modern psychic researchers would have belittled the Murray telepathic experiences on the basis that they were not controlled under laboratory conditions, and Murray acknowledged that his informal experiments "belong to the pre-statistical stage of psychic research, when experiments were treated almost as a parlor game." However, according to Robert H. Ashby, author of *The Guidebook for the Study of Psychical Research* (1972), "the Murray tests, while not entirely quantifiable [measurable by modern standards], are still probably the most impressive demonstrations of telepathy on record."

The first study of telepathy in the United States was made by Dr. J. E. Coover at Stanford University in 1912, and was financed by an endowment of $50,000, a sizable sum in those days. Based on English patterns, he conducted about 14,000 card-guessing trials, using only the numerical cards of the deck. Later researchers have criticized Coover's results on the basis that they failed to consider the important element of possible clairvoyance in relation to chance.

The most prominent amateur American psychic before telepathy was studied by the researchers at Duke University was Upton Sinclair, the novelist and sociologist, who recorded the astonishing accounts of his own experiences in *Mental Radio* (1930). After his wife Mary discovered that she could transfer her thoughts to others, they undertook a long series of tests. Mrs. Sinclair was the receiver (percipient) and her husband and other persons acted as senders (agents).

Mr. Sinclair or a friend would gaze at and think of a simple drawing, and in another room his wife would attempt to visualize the drawing and reproduce it on paper. Considerable concentration was necessary. Distance was apparently no obstacle, as experiments with her brother-in-law, forty miles away, were also successful.

Out of almost three hundred tests, Mr. Sinclair claimed that 23 percent were fully successful, 53 percent partly successful, and only the remaining 24 percent complete failures. It is probable that some of the successes were due to clairvoyance rather than telepathy. Since these experiments, like those of Professor Murray, predated the introduction of established controls, Sinclair's results must be accepted at face value.

Recently, however, a new turn in telepathy research has taken place, due to the possibility discovered by the Duke investigators that the results of their telepathy experiments were produced by clairvoyance.

Many persons unfamiliar with the field of parapsychology fail to distinguish between telepathy and clairvoyance, the most familiar subdivisons of ESP. These terms were in general use long before the term "extrasensory perception" was introduced and became accepted.

Telepathy involves communication between the minds of two individuals, the sender or agent and the receiver or percipient. The latter must learn what the former is thinking about. This means that the thoughts of the agent become known to the percipient, whether the receiver wishes it or not and without his making any effort at communication.

Clairvoyance differs from telepathy in that only one person is involved. The percipient can become aware of an event or the characteristics of an object without the involvement of a second person acting as a transmitter (in telepathy, the agent).

Dr. Ian Stevenson of the University of Virginia has explained the relationship between sender and receiver in telepathy: "A relationship, not just an individual, is necessary for such experiences to occur. . . . It is nevertheless certain that in many instances the agent was *not* thinking of the percipient and yet the latter somehow gained knowledge about his situation."

In his *Telepathic Impressions* (1970), which reported thirty-five previously unpublished cases, Dr. Stevenson emphasizes that such experiences happen more often to some persons than to others. "But even for these more gifted percipients," he declares, "the experiences tended to occur more often with certain individuals as agents than with others, again pointing up the importance of relationships rather than of specific individual persons." The telepathic cases described later in this chapter between Mark Twain and his wife and Luther Burbank and both his mother and sister show this factor.

However, some cases that at first glance seem to be rather clear instances of telepathy may instead be examples of clairvoyance. As Dr. Stevenson points out:

> The percipient's mind may scan the environment for his or her loved ones and, when this is detected, tunes in and brings more details to the surface of the consciousness. In such cases agent focusing could be a coincidental and inconsequential feature arising from the fact that the agent, when in distress, would naturally think of loved ones who would wish to help . . . . In other experiences, however, the activity of the agent may play an important and decisive role.

The difference between a telepathy and a clairvoyance experiment is clearly stated by Herbert Greenhouse:

> In a test for telepathy, the agent or sender tries to beam his thoughts to the subject's [receiver's] mind. In clairvoyance tests the agent may handle the object, but he does not know what it is. If it is a playing card or a picture, it is laid face down, put in an envelope, or otherwise hidden from his view.

Telepathy was most emphasized in the early period of *psi* investigation at Duke University, and it has therefore received the widest popular attention. In more recent decades, however, the experimental work in parapsychology has been preponderantly concerned with clairvoyance, and as parapsychology has advanced as a science, the basic similarity between the two processes has become more and more apparent.

Drs. Rhine and Pratt, writing in 1957, stated, "it now seems doubtful whether they are two different processes after all. . . . At any rate, it would be difficult to offer any specific fundamental difference between these two types of ESP." These authorities, however, offer a warning:

> Most of the cases of telepathy reported are open to interpre-

> tation in terms of either telepathy or clairvoyance, but as should be expected, most people having such experiences think of them as telepathic. . . . Even though telepathy is both more popular, more familiar, and more readily acceptable even to the general scientist, it has proved to be a much more difficult phenomenon to investigate and isolate from clairvoyance experimentally.

The term "mind reading," a synonym for telepathy, has little more than historical interest today because of changing ideas about the concept of mind. However, something should be said about mind reading as it is done on the stage. Performers who can mystify the public with demonstrations of so-called telepathy do not on that account have any claim to psychic ability. Even though they often make a show of waiting for "impressions," their demonstations have nothing in common with ESP experiments. No magician could produce his results under the controlled conditions of the standard ESP tests, but on the stage he can dictate his own conditions and devise his own routines.

In the most elementary telepathy tricks the performer walks among the audience asking people to hold up articles like wallets and watches, while on the stage a blindfolded assistant calls out the names of the objects selected. This is usually done by means of a code. The performer gives his partner innocent-sounding encouragements, such as "Come on," "Hurry up," "Surely you know what this is." The words he uses, even the inflection of his voice, can convey the information to his partner. Sometimes, when blindfold is not used, a silent code is employed, depending on bodily postures and slight gesture, but long practice is needed for that. Simpler and just as mystifying to the audience is the use of a small concealed radio transmitter.

Some telepathy tricks depend upon what magicians call "forcing." A member of the audience picks a card or number, thinking he has made a free choice, and immediately the assistant calls out correctly what he has chosen. The simplest methods of forcing depend upon sleight of hand. The victim cuts a pack and picks off the top card from the bottom cut. In between the two actions there is a momentary pause in which the performer, while asking the victim if he is satisfied with the cut, places a prearranged card on top of the pile.

The performer also knows by experience that in certain arrangements of cards one or two particular cards are nearly always selected in preference to the rest. These predictions are not certain, but a few failures add to the impression of genuineness.

Performers who "accomplish" telepathic feats have always interested investigators. One of the most famous English psychic researchers, Dr. S. G. Soal, who specialized in telepathic investigation, made a comprehensive study of Frederick Marion, a particularly adept stage performer. Marion specialized in locating hidden articles and in identifying playing cards chosen by members of his audiences. Picking up clues had become second nature to him after years of practice, and he could hardly say himself exactly how he did it.

He claimed psychic powers, but his methods were apparent to those who knew his technique. In a series of ingeniously planned tests, Soal showed that Marion depended chiefly upon the subject's face. He was successful even when the subject's body was hidden behind a screen, but once the face was covered Marion's guesses were no better than could have occurred by chance.

After analyzing the results of twenty-four test performances, Soal reached the conclusion that Marion had the power to locate objects in a room where he could observe the reactions of half a dozen or so people and that he failed when he was alone in a room or when his subject was concealed from view in a movable upright box. In his report, *Preliminary Studies of a Vaudeville Telepathist,* published in 1937 by the University of London Council for Psychical Investigation, Soal commented that "Marion probably derives his information from head movements and changes in facial expression when the subjects are seated."

In his book on occult and psychic phenomena, Milbourne Christopher, the famous illusionist, makes this comment: "The professional thought reader is actually aware of the changes in breathing, tensions and relaxations, and varying positions of the fingers, hands, and feet of his subjects when he works without contact." Almost all so-called thought readers work without touching their subjects.

As noted previously, telepathy in action, in contrast to experimental situations, most often involves a personal relationship. As a part of Ian Stevenson's study of telepathic experiences, he analyzed 160 cases published by three of the most noted organizations up to 1967 as well as those in *Phantasms of the Living,* one of the earliest collections of such cases, which was published in 1886.

In the largest number of cases, almost two thirds (62 percent) of the agents (senders) and percipients (receivers) were members of the same immediate family. Fourteen percent were husbands and wives, 15 percent siblings, and 34 percent parents and children. Twenty-eight percent were friends and acquaintances, 7 percent relatives (cousins, grandparents, in-laws, etc.), and only 2 percent strangers. Dr. Stevenson interprets these figures as evidence of the role of emotional factors in ESP.

This is to be expected. People who are close to one another will naturally be "attuned" to each other, and the receiver will more readily pick up a telepathic thought. For example, when a family member, relative, or close friend is seriously ill, a person's thoughts will be focused upon him or her, and a telepathic exchange may take place. In Stevenson's 160 cases, approximately 40 percent involved dying. Cases classified by him as serious—accidents, danger, and the like—made up another 40 percent. Only about 20 percent were characterized as "not serious," such as good news, expected arrivals, and the like, leading to the conclusion that pleasant and happy events—births, marriages, business successes, etc.—do not often figure in telepathic cases.

Mark Twain was perhaps the greatest American humorist of the latter part of the nineteenth century, but he had a serious side, which he hid from all but his family and closest friends. He was interested in telepathy and was a longtime member of the Society for Psychical Research (London). Twain wrote occasional articles on what he called "mental telegraphy" for them and recounted what he regarded as telepathic experiences of his own. His principal biographer, Albert Bigelow Paine, knew him so well that his book about Twain filled three large volumes. Noted Paine:

> In thought transference, especially, he had a frank interest—an interest awakened and kept alive by certain phenomena—psychic manifestations we call them now. In his association with Mrs. Clemens it not infrequently happened that one spokethe other's thought or perhaps a long procrastinated letter to a friend would bring an answer as quickly as mailed.

The phenomenon of "crossing letters" came about many times. In a periodical article, Twain wrote of it:

> We are always talking about letters crossing each other, for that is one of the very commonest accidents of our lives. We call it "accident," but perhaps we misname it. We have the instinct a dozen times a year that the letter we are writing is going to cross the other's letter. . . .
>
> When I sit down to write a letter under the coercion of a strong impulse, I consider that the other person is supplying the thoughts to me, and that I am merely writing from dictation. . . .

When the Comstock Lode, the richest known American silver deposit, was discovered near Virginia City, Nevada, in 1873, Twain's publisher, the American Publishing Company of Hartford, suggested that a book on the subject would be well-timed. Twain thought that a journalist named William H. Wright, who was on the spot, would be a good person to write it. After he had written a letter with the suggestion to Wright, Twain put it aside until he could talk more fully to his publisher.

A week later, an unsolicited letter arrived from Virginia City. Before opening it, Twain remarked to a visiting relative, "Now I will do a miracle. I will tell you everything this letter contains—date, signature, and all—without breaking the seal. It is from Mr. Wright, of Virginia City, Nevada, and is dated the second of March, seven days ago. Mr. Wright proposes to make a book about the silver mines and asks what I, as a friend, think of the idea. He says his subjects are to be so and so, their order and sequence so and so, and he will close with a history of the chief feature of the book, 'The Great Bonanza.' "

Twain then opened the letter and confirmed his "knowledge" of its contents; they corresponded exactly with his own letter, which he had written but not mailed a week before. Mr. Wright, the editor of the *Territorial Enterprise* in Virginia City, had been asked by some of the local citizens who had become millionaires to write a book on the Big Bonanza, and Wright had worked on the manuscript in his spare time. The book, titled *The History of the Big Bonanza*, was eventually published in Hartford in 1896. Twain's "mental telegraphy" obviously functioned!

Another prominent practitioner of telepathy was Luther Burbank, famous as a plant breeder. He had a strong mystic side to his character, and it was one that he cultivated. During his boyhood his mother, Mrs. Olive Burbank, had a knowledge of events about which she spoke before they happened, such as Luther's breaking his arm and the death of his grandfather.

After her son moved to California, Mrs. Burbank visited him, and in tests before representatives of the

University of California she was able, seven times out of ten, to receive messages sent to her telepathically. "My mother's brain," Burbank once remarked, "was both a transmitting and receiving radio-telephone instrument."

Burbank inherited his mother's ability to send and receive telepathic communications. Mrs. Burbank lived to be more than ninety-five years of age and was in poor health the last years of her life. "During these years," Burbank wrote, "I often wished to summon my sister Emma, with whom she lived. On such occasions I never had to write, telephone or telegraph to her. Instead, I send her messages telepathically, and each time she arrived in Santa Rosa, where I live, on the next train."

After Burbank moved to California his eastern friends quite naturally wanted to be kept informed of his progress, particularly when he began to develop new plants and fruits. A special friend wired him, asking him to telegraph news, since mail service in the 1870s was slow. Burbank's reaction to this request was unusual; he sent the answer across the continent, he averred, by thought waves. His friend "tuned in" and wrote back to thank him for the information.

In a 1923 magazine article, the scientist expanded on his belief in telepathy:

> A few years ago, such incidents would have been attributed to insanity or the supernatural. I relate them now not because I believe my mother was and my sister Emma and I are supernormal, but because I am convinced we are not. I believe we all have been broadcasting and receiving from the beginning of human thought. Those who can send messages

to particular persons differ from the others only in that they can direct their thought waves where they wish them to go.

Thomas Edison, America's most famous inventor who patented over a thousand inventions, was another man of science who was interested in both telepathy and spiritualism, which he approached from a detached and unemotional view.

Edison admitted that he received assistance in perfecting some of his inventions, such as the electric battery, from Bert Reese, a noted contemporary clairvoyant. Joseph Dunninger, the famous mentalist who was a friend of Edison, once remarked that inventors in general were often intrigued with telepathy since they "receive impressions or gain ideas that seem to come from some outside force." (Chester F. Carlson, the inventor of the Xerox process of photographic reproduction, admitted that the idea came to him through telepathy, and on his death he willed a part of his fortune to psychic research.)

Although Edison was unsuccessful in demonstrating his telepathic powers in formal experiments, he never lost interest in it, and a psychiatrist has suggested that the great man's deafness and his well-known habit of napping between long hours of laboratory work made him receptive to telepathic impressions.

A difficulty in recognizing and experimenting in telepathy is that science still does not have a clear-cut answer as to whether the transmission of mental images without known means of communication is possible.

Skeptics maintain that telepathy smacks of the supernatural. They say it reminds them of spiritualism with mediums receiving messages in a "spooky" atmosphere. Certainly it is still one of the most mysterious of the ESP phenomena.

CHAPTER 6

Clairvoyance

The word "clairvoyance" derives from two French words, the adjective *clair* ("clear") and the present participle *voyant,* ("seeing")—in other words "clear seeing." Definitions in dictionaries vary in explanatory information. In the American Heritage Dictionary clairvoyance is defined as "the supposed power to perceive things that are out of the natural range of human senses, attributed to certain individuals." The Merriam-Webster Third International Dictionary defines it more completely: "the act or power professed by certain persons of discerning objects hidden from sight or at a great distance." A simpler definition, however, might be " 'seeing' objects or events that cannot be perceived normally."

Though the term literally means "clear seeing," in reality it has nothing to do with vision. As Dr. Rhine points out, "clairvoyant impressions may be in the form of visual imagery, but they may also be of other types as well. . . . Any direct apprehension of external objects is clairvoyance if the senses are not involved."

An example of spontaneous (nonlaboratory) clairvoyance cited by Dr. Rhine will make clear what is meant by the word. *Phantasms of the Living,* a collection of studies by three founders of the Society for Psychical Research (London), reported the experience of a child who had a vision of her mother lying ill in their home. The child, a girl of ten, was walking along a country lane reading a geometry book, when suddenly her surroundings faded away, and she saw her mother lying apparently dead on the floor of an unused room at home. The vision was very clear; the child even noticed a lace-bordered handkerchief lying on the floor a short distance from her mother.

The experience was so real that, instead of going straight home, the girl went at once to the home of the family doctor and convinced him that he should go home with her. She could not explain her reasons to him, for her mother had apparently been in good health and was supposed to have been away from home that day.

When the doctor and the girl arrived at the house, they met the father going in. Seeing the doctor, the father immediately asked, "Who is ill?" The child told him that her mother was ill, and at once led them to the unused room. There on the floor lay the mother, exactly as she had been seen in the vision. The lace-bordered handkerchief lay a short distance away. The mother was found to be suffering from a heart attack, and the doctor assured them that if he had not arrived when he did, she would not have recovered.

It was only when the episode was over that the father discovered that his wife had been taken ill after the child had left the house. None of the servants knew of the sudden illness. No one had seen the events take place.

"Hence," wrote Dr. Rhine, "telepathy seems an unlikely explanation. The girl's vision of the scene appears to have been one of clairvoyance or the extrasensorial knowledge of objective events."

The relation of clairvoyance to telepathy has been pointed out in Chapter 5, but it is also closely related to precognition, particularly when it involves a foreknowledge of objects or events such as disasters.

Like telepathy, clairvoyance was first thought to be dependent on hypnosis. Many hypnotists reported that they were able to direct a hypnotized subject to project himself mentally to a distant scene and bring back a reliable account of specific happenings or other items of information, which tallied with later verification. But eventually both telepathy and clairvoyance were proved without recourse to hypnosis.

As pointed out previously, when Duke University began experimental work in the 1930s, telepathy and clairvoyance were of equal interest, but the latter took the lead and continued thereafter to hold it. At Duke there was a practical reason for preferring clairvoyance as a starting point in the investigation of psychic abilities. The elements involved in the experiments were simple, and there was only one subject to deal with and keep under observation. Only the target object had to be hidden.

During the first three years, experimenters at the

laboratory conducted enough tests to conclude that extrasensory perception of the clairvoyant type had been established. The tests with the Zener (ESP) cards, they believed, eliminated the element of chance.

The most conclusive test, which became a classic in the field, was conducted from August, 1933, to March, 1934. In this distance test, the subject (percipient) was Hubert E. Pearce, a divinity student who had worked with the laboratory for more than a year. The tests were administered by J. Gaither Pratt, at that time a graduate student in the Duke psychology department.

Pearce was sent to a building a hundred yards away from that in which Pratt handled the target cards. The cards were hidden one at a time at one-minute intervals, and their order was not recorded until after the full run of twenty-five trials. Throughout the run the cards were kept face down, and Pearce, in the other building, recorded his guesses as he made them. Duplicate records of both the cards and the calls made double independent checking possible. With the completion of a planned series of three hundred guesses under these conditions over a six-day period, the results were so highly and uniformly successful that it was obvious the results could not be due to chance.

In three hundred guesses sixty hits could be expected on the basis of pure chance, but the odds were 1 million to 1 against 119 hits occurring by chance alone! Dr. Rhine then joined Mr. Pratt as an observer in another series, and it validated the previous results.

If any doubt remained about the existence of clairvoyance after the Duke experiments—several others were undertaken after Pearce-Pratt both at Duke and by institutions and organizations in both the United States and Europe—they were completely banished when Pavel Stepanek, the Czech specialist, carried through his extraordinary achievements, which are described in Chapter 4.

Experiences suggesting that mind can go beyond space are abundant. Clairvoyant occurrences, and those of precognition, almost stretch the bounds of human credulity, and many persons still refuse to believe and accept them.

The classic case was that of the eighteenth-century Swedish scientist, philosopher, and theologian, Emanuel Swedenborg. One day in 1759, he was visiting a country house near Göteborg. Returning from the terrace, he appeared pale and upset, and he told other guests that a dangerous fire had just broken out at Södermalm, his hometown three hundred miles distant near Stockholm. A short time later he added that the house of one of his friends was already reduced to ashes and that his own was in danger from the spreading flames. After about four hours he told his friends, with great relief, "Thank God! The fire is put out, the third door from my house."

When the provincial governor learned of Swedenborg's mental image, he inquired about the details. The scientist described the fire precisely, how it had begun, how long it had continued, and how its progress had been stopped. Three days later, a messenger brought letters describing the fire; the details were exactly as Swedenborg had described them. This incident was later confirmed by three prominent men.

Swedenborg's clairvoyant ability functioned in several other instances. For example, the widow of the Dutch ambassador to Sweden received a very substantial bill from a jeweler for a silver service that her husband had purchased from him before his death. Because he had always been very prompt in meeting his financial obligations, his wife questioned the bill. She had learned of Swedenborg's "observation" of the fire, so she sought his assistance. Within three days he informed her that the receipt for payment was to be found in the drawer of a bureau located in an upstairs room of her home. It was, he said, in a secret compartment. Though the woman had no knowledge of any secret drawer, that is where she found the lost receipt.

The literature of psychic research is full of confirmed occurrences of clairvoyance. The files of the Parapsychology Laboratory at Duke include literally hundreds of such incidents. Those of three of Dr. Rhine's personal friends—and vouched for by him—are worth recounting in his own words as more or less typical of spontaneous clairvoyance:

> A psychologist friend once told me that his son, while living in Java many years ago, had a vivid dream of a funeral procession passing through his home town in South Carolina. The dream made such an impression upon him that he wrote home to inquire if it meant anything. The time of the dream roughly corresponded with the funeral of his mother, who had died unexpectedly.

A prominent minister and his wife once stopped at the Parapsychology Laboratory to relate a similar experience. When they were traveling in Switzerland some years ago the wife one day had a sudden, unaccountable impression that her sister in Chicago was dead. The idea was so unreasonable, however, that she decided not to mention it. A few days later she had an equally strong conviction that her sister was being buried. This time she told her husband, and he made a note of her impressions, although he was doubtful of their accuracy. When letters caught up with them they discovered that she had been right about what happened to her sister and also about the days on which the death and the funeral had occurred.

Another instance was reported to me by the president of a large university. It was once his duty to notify an American couple of the sudden death of their son in China. On hearing the unhappy news the father turned to the mother and said, "You were right." A few days earlier she had told her husband that she was sure their son was dead.

During the years of both World Wars, many paranormal experiences were reported. In such cases the wife, mother, or fiancée of a man in the armed forces received an impression of his injury or death coincident with the event itself. In most instances this knowledge came to the recipient over a great expanse of land, mountain, and sea.

A unique form of clairvoyance is object reading or psychometry. Some psychic persons, when given an object to hold, are able to describe events and persons connected with the object. For example, while holding a piece of jewelry which has been worn regularly by another person, a psychic can receive pictures in his mind.

Peter Hurkos, the famous psychic, once became unconscious during one of his consultations, had extreme difficulty in breathing and was rushed to a hospital. After four hours in a coma he revived, and the first thing he noticed was an unusual ring worn by one of the nurses attending him. He asked her to let him hold the ring, and said, "The person this ring belonged to is dead." He continued describing specific incidents and details of past events involving the former owner.

The doctors and nurses were so fascinated by this that they gathered around his bed, and Hurkos began to relate past incidents concerning each one. He was given a brain test (electroencephalogram) and in the medical report was labeled as possessing "physic symptoms!"

The account in Chapter 2 of the psychic in New York State who located two children kidnapped by their divorced father in North Carolina by focusing on their photographs is an example of psychometry.

Psychometry can also be used to perceive events in the past, as a form of retrocognition (see Chapter 7).

Dowsing, the search for underground water or minerals by the use of a rod, appears to be an example of the mind's clairvoyant faculty in action. It is sometimes called divining, and the object used is termed a divining rod. The agent is now called a dowser, as is the person performing, although the origin of this term is unknown. The device used is usually a forked twig, though in modern times it may be a metal rod or a pendulum.

Dowsing is of very ancient origin, but the first authenticated evidence of the practice, with a forked stick, comes from medieval Germany, and is related in *De re metallica,* a guide for locating minerals and ores.

Differences of opinion have always existed as to whether dowsing is accomplished by physical or mental means. If the former is correct, some sort of ray or electric or magnetic power reacts to the rod and the material being sought. Nineteenth-century investigators of this phenomenon believed that the movement of the twig or rod was due to unconscious muscular action on the part of the dowser. They found, however, that the rod frequently exerted a tremendous force beyond the will or control of the dowser and frequently in direct opposition to his will or belief. Psychical researchers are familiar with this kind of involuntary muscular action, which is the same type of motion that causes a table to tip in séances or the pointer (or planchette, a triangular piece of wood mounted on a base) to move across the face of a Ouija board to spell out a message supposedly sent by a spirit. However, it was established that none of the dowsers studied were able to produce the phenomenon by such muscular action alone.

The latter fact indicated that the finding of water or mineral deposits could be attributed to some form of clairvoyance, and the question became "How did the knowledge of when to probe a certain area with the object in hand enter the dowser's mind? "

To parapsychologists, dowsing is a combination of movement with some extrasensory guidance in the discovery of the location of the water or mineral being sought. In the most familiar type of practice the dowser is asked to find a suitable location for a well. He takes a forked twig by the two small ends and, holding it in such a way that it swings easily and with slight pressure, he walks over the ground until the rod swings downward. A dowser usually believes he is exerting no influence on the twig and that it is responding to forces given off from the underground material he is seeking.

In spite of the widespread and still active practice of dowsing, the operation of the clairvoyant function, if it exists, has not yet been thoroughly and satisfactorily explained. Controlled experiments have been undertaken with some success when the dowser involved had confidence and was aware of the possibility of using clairvoyant power. Some of the exploratory experiments in dowsing have been carried out in laboratories using hidden coins, parallel to locating mineral deposits.

In the 1920s, William Barrett, a British physicist, and Theodore Besterman, an investigator for the Society for Psychical Research, studied the activities of several English dowsers out of doors, and with two of the most effective dowsers performed experiments such as locating a coin hidden under a covering of one of forty-five chairs, with notable success.

A group of parapsychologists from the American Society for Psychical Research under Dr. Gardner Murphy conducted outdoor tests with twenty-seven dowsers and two professional geologists in 1949, seeking to locate underground water in Maine. The scientists proved more successful than the professional dowsers, and the experiment appeared to prove only that unconscious muscular action was involved. Many geologists attribute the success of dowsers to the fact that if one drills deeply enough in most places, water will be found.

The most successful American dowser was Henry Gross, a Maine game warden, who attracted the attention of the historical novelist and Pulitzer Prize winner Kenneth Roberts, a writer noted principally for his *Northwest Passage.* Roberts became so intrigued with Gross's water probes that he wrote two books: *Henry Gross and His Dowsing Rod,* describing his subject's methods in detail, and *The Seventh Sense,* a study of the practice. Gross admitted that his rod often dipped at the very spot where he had already decided that water would be found; perhaps, however, this was intuition. Nevertheless, he was equally successful in probing at random, and once located a lost bracelet buried in the wet sand of a beach.

Nonetheless, from whatever mental, physical, or psychic force, effective dowsing is a fact of contemporary life. Prospectors working for petroleum companies use metal rods in determining where to drill for oil reserves and locating previously laid pipelines, and mining companies attempt to locate veins of the newer radioactive metals such as uranium through dowsing methods. When maps are unavailable, city sanitation department workers frequently use dowsing methods to locate previously laid sewer pipes, as do public utility companies in locating electric and telephone wire conduits, in order to plan their work.

The most recent unusual use of dowsing was by United States Marine engineers in Vietnam in 1967, where they used coat hangers as rods to locate land mines, buried weapons, and enemy tunnels. The rods, bent into L shapes, were held in each hand pointing forward as the dowser walked. When over a mine or other buried object, they swung apart forming a straight line. This method was taught at the Marine training school at Quantico, Virginia.

The specific role of clairvoyance in dowsing, however, remains to be determined.

CHAPTER 7

Precognition

Precognition is defined as "knowledge of something in advance of its occurrence." In its psychic sense, it is "knowledge of a future event or situation through extrasensory means." In parapsychology, as used by Dr. Rhine, precognition is "cognition of a future event which could not be known through rational inference." In less technical terms, it is simply the perception of a future event by ESP.

On the question of validity, Dr. Rhine has stated:

> To qualify as a genuine instance of precognition an experience must refer to a coming event to an extent that is more than merely accidental; it must identify a future happening that could not have been inferred as about to occur, and finally, it must refer to an event that could not have been brought about as a consequence of the prediction.

True psychic precognition involves premonition, a forewarning in advance of an occurrence, a presentiment of the future in which there is often an element of anxiety over coming events.

What is now termed precognition has been familiarly known throughout history as prophecy. In all ages, men have been awestruck by the power of the prophet to dip into the future and to announce what is going to happen. People looked upon this ability as not of this world, but divine and supernatural, even frightening.

Prophecy has always been considered both uncanny and unreal, and the prophets in the Bible used it as a threat. Doom was inescapable to those who did not accept the omens and signs that forecast the future.

The principal element in precognition is time. In such experiences the ordinary barriers are apparently broken down. All spontaneous *psi* occurrences go beyond the boundaries of time as well as space. A person who has such an experience often does not know whether or not the event that has come to his consciousness has happened yet. This is especially likely to be the case where distant events are involved.

On the eve of the development of parapsychology at Duke University, a book that made history in the field of psychic research was published in London. In *An Experiment with Time* (1927), John W. Dunne introduced the theory that the "now" can be regarded as existing partly in the past and extending partly into the future. Dunne was not a psychic researcher but an engineer. A series of his remarkable precognition dreams led him to experiment with them. When he realized that he was seeing in these dreams events that actually occurred the following day or even several days later, he thought at first that there must be something eccentric in his relation to time.

Dunne recorded his dreams, both personal and impersonal, in detail immediately on awakening, and afterward noted what proportion came true. He finally concluded that his experience was normal and that any investigator could duplicate it. With the more recent parapsychological experiments, Dunne's theory has been reinforced as well as revised, but psychics have found that his pioneer study, within its limitations, may be considered a landmark.

How do these precognitive experiences unfold? They crop up out of nowhere in the lives of ordinary men and women. "They just come to me suddenly" is the usual explanation. They simply seize the mind in a mysterious, unaccountable way. ESP research is still being conducted on this factor.

Precognition most often operates in dreams. The Maimonides Medical Center Dream Laboratory has recognized the *psi* factor in scores of controlled sleep experiments, and the director, Dr. Stanley Krippner, feels that precognition in dreams is a scientifically proved phenomenon.

Individuals possessing the faculty of precognition often make predictions that involve themselves, family members, or acquaintances. According to Hans Holzer:

> Personal predictions are made by people in all walks of life. Some of these impressions of future events come while the psychic subject is awake, some while he is in the dream state when the bonds between conscious and unconscious mind are looser and the door to perception ajar.

One of the most frequent types of precognition concerns death. The psychic person sees the event as it will actually happen (or is happening) and can predict it precisely. History abounds in such occurrences. Two of the most widely known concern President Abraham Lincoln and Mark Twain.

Despite his famous sense of humor and fondness for jokes, Lincoln has always been characterized by his many biographers as basically a melancholy man. His perpetual look of sadness was his most prominent feature, and his frequent dreams were invariably of unhappy events, for he had a foreboding of disaster. A very good friend from Illinois days, Ward Lamon, recounted a conversation between Lincoln and his wife in the White House shortly before his assassination. They were talking of dreams, and he told her of one he had had:

> "About ten days ago," [Lincoln] said, "I began to dream. There seemed to be a death-like stillness about me. Then I heard subdued sobs, as if a number of people were weeping. I thought I left my bed and wandered downstairs. I went from room to room; no living person was in sight, but the same mournful sounds of distress met me as I passed along.
>
> "I was puzzled and alarmed. What could be the meaning of all this? Determined to find the cause of a state of things so mysterious and shocking, I kept on until I arrived at the East Room, which I entered. Before me was a catafalque on which rested a corpse wrapped in funeral vestments, the face covered. Around it were stationed soldiers who were acting as guards. A throng of people were weeping pitifully.
>
> " 'Who is dead in the White House?' I demanded of one of the soldiers. 'The President,' was his answer. 'He was killed by an assassin!' Then came a loud burst of grief from the crowd, which awoke me from my dream. I slept no more that night, and although it was only a dream I have been strangely annoyed by it ever since."

After the murder of her husband beside her in the Ford Theater box, the first words Mary Lincoln spoke were, "His dream was prophetic."

Albert Bigelow Paine, Mark Twain's biographer, recounted a precognitional experience concerning Twain and his brother, who lived with him in St. Louis while both worked on Mississippi River boats. Mark (then Samuel Clemens, his real name) was a pilot, and his experiences in those days resulted in his book *Life on the Mississippi* and formed the background for his two classics, *Tom Sawyer* and *Huckleberry Finn.*

One night while Sam was sleeping on shore downriver from St. Louis, where his brother Henry was to board the *Pennsylvania,* a passenger vessel, he had a vivid dream. Wrote Paine:

> He saw Henry, a corpse, lying in a metallic burial case in a sitting room, supported by two chairs. On his breast lay a bouquet of white flowers with a single crimson bloom in the center. When he awoke, it was morning, but the dream was so vivid that he believed it real. . . . He rushed to the parlor and found with joy that it was empty.

The next day he started north and, as usual, expected to pass his brother's boat and wave to him. When his own vessel touched at a port, a voice from the landing shouted, "The *Pennsylvania* has blown up just below Memphis! One hundred and fifty lives lost!" Nothing further could be learned there, but that evening at another port, Twain learned that Henry had escaped injury. Still farther north, a newspaper extra brought news that he had been scalded beyond recovery when the boilers of the burning boat had exploded.

When Twain finally arrived at Memphis, he located the house where his brother's body lay. Paine continued:

> The coffins provided for the dead were of unpainted wood, but the ladies of Memphis had made up a fund of sixty dollars and bought a metallic case for Henry. Entering the room, Sam saw his brother lying exactly as he had seen him in his dream, lacking only the bouquet of white flowers with its crimson center—a detail made complete while he stood there, for at that moment an elderly lady came in with a large white bouquet and in the center was a single red rose.

Many dreams prove accurate down to the smallest detail. Strangely enough, an estimated one half to three quarters of death predictions prove to be true.

That of Emanuel Swedenborg, who "saw" the fire in his hometown when he was three hundred miles away, was almost unique. Twenty-three years later, John Wesley, the founder of Methodism, wrote Swedenborg and proposed a meeting with him on March 29, 1772.

The philosopher, who was then eighty-four, declined politely, explaining that he could accept no engagements so far in advance because his death was scheduled for that day.

And die he did, on that date, from natural causes.

Such a personal forecast is fairly common in psychic persons.

Not all predictions concern private persons. Both amateur and professional psychics foresee catastrophes of all types—local, national, and worldwide. They may concern the fates of prominent men and women or, increasingly more often, natural disasters and events.

Many of these forecasts are arrived at through seeing visions while crystal gazing, technically characterized as "scrying," "a method of receiving psychic information of the past, present, and future through images in a reflecting surface." The psychic gazes into the ball until pictures are received. Traditionally a device of gypsies, its use has spread.

Differences of opinion exist as to whether the technique is an occult or a psychic one. As a result, the predictions of many crystal gazers are inaccurate, and often the scryers themselves are charlatans, Even so, every year, scores of psychics and occultists from all over the world publish their forecasts of events that can be anticipated during the coming year. Few of the predictions are happy, and prophecies of natural and personal disasters abound. By the theory of probability, some are certain to be exact, but the percentage of error, even among trained and conscientious psychics, is often high.

The most prominent American psychic who uses a crystal ball is Jeane Dixon, whose autobiography *My Life and Prophecies* (1969) claims that she has predicted many public events: the assassination of President John Kennedy and the name of his killer, two years before it occurred; the assassination of Mahatma Gandhi; the deaths in plane accidents of movie star Carole Lombard and United Nations Secretary General Dag Hammarskjöld; the suicide of film star Marilyn Monroe; the partition of India in 1947; and the takeover of Communism in China. She also predicted that Secretary of State John Foster Dulles would die in the spring of 1959, and in 1952, looking forward more than a decade, she forecast that serious race rioting would bloody American streets in 1963 and 1964. All through the 1960s there were riots in this country. She says that she "saw" the assassination of Robert Kennedy and predicted the death of Martin Luther King both at the same time.

Conversely, since some of Mrs. Dixon's forecasts have failed to occur, she admits that she is not infallible. (Her prediction that President Kennedy's widow would not remarry was due to be published in her newspaper column the very day that Jackie Kennedy became Mrs. Onassis. Editors hastily deleted it before publication.) Moreover, many of Mrs. Dixon's predictions have been duplicated by lesser known psychics.

Persons possessing psychic powers often predict natural disasters and catastrophes. For example, the 1971 California earthquakes are reported to have been foreseen by at least two dozen people. Americans were told of the droughts and famines in African countries in the early 1970s, far in advance of their occurrence. The droughts struck in 1973.

Any consideration of this subject must include two astounding and well-known examples of precognition, the sinking of the *Titanic* in 1912 and the coal slide in Aberfan, Wales, in 1966. The validity of the predictions of these two events has been upheld by authorities.

One of the greatest of all sea disasters was the sinking of the liner *Titanic* with a loss of 1,500 lives after it crashed into an iceberg in the North Atlantic south of Newfoundland on the night of April 14–15, 1912. The

Titanic was the fastest ship afloat at the time and was on her maiden voyage. She was thought to be unsinkable and was carrying many notables among her more than 2,000 passengers. The ship was attempting to break the speed record.

William T. Stead, an English journalist who was active in spiritualism, predicted the disaster in which he later lost his life. Many years before, he wrote an imaginative article, published in the *Pall Mall Gazette,* about a large ship that sank in the mid-Atlantic. The story was intended to show what might happen if ships fail to take safety precautions before sailing. At the end of the article was this warning: "This is exactly what might take place and that will take place if liners are sent to sea short of boats."

In 1892, Stead wrote another article in the *Review of Reviews,* of which he was editor. In this story a steamship collides with an iceberg in the Atlantic and its sole surviving passenger is rescued by a liner called the *Majestic.* Later there was an actual ship by that name, and its captain was Edward J. Smith, who was the captain of the *Titanic* in 1912.

Two decades later, Stead's life was tied to the *Titanic,* almost as if he were a victim of destiny being irresistibly pulled toward the fate he had outlined in his stories. This became evident when, in 1910, he gave a lecture in London in which he dramatically pictured himself in a shipwreck floundering in the water and calling for help. Without realizing it, he was a doomed victim of his imagination, and perhaps unconsciously haunted by what friends called a death wish.

He visited a noted London psychic, Count Louis Hamon (later known as Cheiro), at the time the *Titanic* was under construction. Hamon warned him that harm would come to him from water and to stay away from the sea.

Later, in mid-1911, the psychic wrote Stead with a warning that "travel will be dangerous in the month of April, 1912." Shortly thereafter, another psychic told Stead that he would be going to America—a surprise because he had no such plans—and also that he saw a huge ship but only half of the ship. "When one will be able to see it in its whole length," the psychic said, "it is perhaps then that you will go on your journey." The *Titanic* was then only half completed.

The prediction came true when Stead was asked by United States President William H. Taft to speak at a peace conference, and in spite of warnings by several friends, he boarded the *Titanic* on April 10 almost as if to prove that the warnings had no basis in fact. After all, he undoubtedly reasoned, had not the ship been declared the safest in the world?

Stead was among the 1,500 who drowned.

After the disaster, several seamen reported that they had refused to sign on for the voyage. "I just didn't feel right about it," one of them remarked. A fireman had a premonition of danger and deserted the ship at Queenstown.

After the disaster, many other premonitions were revealed. Prospective passengers had canceled their passages. A London businessman had a disturbing dream a fortnight before the scheduled sailing: He saw the

Titanic "floating on the sea, keel upwards and her passengers and crew swimming around her." The dream was repeated the next night, and he was understandably upset. However, because of the importance of his American business, he was inclined to ignore the dreams. About four days before the sailing date, he received a cable from New York urging him to postpone his trip. This he did, and the unanswered question arises: Did the American who sent the cable also have a premonition about the *Titanic?*

In articles written for the American Society for Psychical Research and printed in its *Journal* from 1960 to 1967, Dr. Ian Stevenson described nineteen cases of reported premonitions within two weeks before the disaster, from England, the United States, Canada, and even Brazil. All the experiences were particularly vivid and real. They were like films projected on the minds of the recipients, who were all terrified and depressed by the awful knowledge that had been revealed to them. In addition, their helplessness in preventing the tragedy was frustrating to them.

The Aberfan disaster on October 21, 1966, was one of the first catastrophes to be investigated in relation to the many premonitions that preceded it. At least sixty persons reported receiving information about the avalanche before it buried 116 schoolchildren and twenty-eight adults under a mountain of coal slag in the Wales village. Half a million tons of coal waste, loosened by two days of heavy rainfall, rumbled, then roared down over the village. A school was buried beneath the moving mountain in a black mass forty feet high, and with it over a hundred small children.

Those who lived in other parts of Britain and had premonitions about the disaster did not know it had occurred until they heard the news on the radio or read of it in newspapers the next morning.

According to Herbert Greenhouse in his *Premonitions: A Leap into the Future* (1971), among those "seeing" the tragedy in advance was a retired seaman living in southwest England. A week before, the seaman began to "feel uneasy, he didn't know why." He said to his wife, "Something terrible is going to happen, and it won't be far from here." The sense of imminent disaster was so strong that he thought about coal dust and drew a human head surrounded by a black background.

Three days later, a man living near London suddenly knew that on Friday there would be a frightful catastrophe; however, he could not pinpoint details. Throughout England, similar warnings were received.

The day before the avalanche, a London television performer suddenly canceled a pretaped comedy show that was to have been broadcast on Saturday. The production was about a Welsh mining village, and the actor had a "feeling" that it shouldn't be on the air. Others later reported receiving exact mental pictures of the coal slide and even of rescue workers digging for bodies. A London woman woke up when she heard the frantic screams of a child who was attempting to escape from a "black, billowing mass."

In the early hours of that fateful Friday, an Englishman living in northwestern England had a dream in which he saw A–B–E–R–F–A–N spelled out in a brilliant light; the word meant nothing to him until he heard a radio broadcast later that day.

When nine-year-old Eryl Jones, who lived in the mining village, woke up on Thursday morning, she said to her mother, "Mummy, let me tell you about my dream last night." Her mother answered, "Darling, I have no time now. Tell me later." But the child replied, "No, Mummy, you must listen. I dreamed I went to school and there was no school there. Something black had come down all over it! "

After the tragedy in which Eryl had died, her mother recalled that she had made a very strange remark a fortnight before: "Mummy, I'm not afraid to die." Her mother had said, "Why do you talk of dying, and you so young? " to which the child repeated, "I'm not afraid to die. I shall be with Peter and June." They were her classmates.

On Friday at 9 A. M., Eryl went to school as usual. As she left, the clock in her house stopped ticking. The mountain moved at 9:30. Trees were uprooted, houses and cottages crumbled, and the school was completely buried under the avalanche. A mass funeral was held on the twenty-fifth and the bodies of the 116 children were buried in a common grave, among them Eryl and her two friends, Peter and June.

Dr. J. C. Barker, a London psychiatrist who was interested in premonitions and was then writing a book called *Scared to Death,* in which he planned to discuss cases he had come across of persons dying at the exact time predicted by fortune tellers and psychics, arrived in Aberfan during the rescue operations. Dr. Barker knew that premonitions of disaster had been common since ancient times. Plagues, fires, tornadoes, earthquakes, all had been seen first in visions and dreams, and he asked himself why, since so many of these premonitions had proved accurate, this foreknowledge had not been used to prevent the disasters, or at least to warn those who later perished.

At the time, Dr. Barker had no knowledge of such forecasts of the Aberfan tragedy, and he asked the science editor of the London *Evening Standard* to make an appeal in his newspaper to those who had received such premonitions. Within a fortnight, seventy-six replies were received, most of them from the London area.

The Psychophysical Research Unit at Oxford made a similar appeal through *The Sun,* another London newspaper. A third journal, *News of the World,* printed the results of an investigation that included interviews. The three surveys resulted in two hundred replies. Dr. Barker discarded some reports and studied sixty in detail, evaluating them with criteria established by a well-known parapsychologist.

Dr. Barker described the individuals who had made these predictions as "human seismographs." As he examined the Aberfan precognition cases, the thought occurred to him that "the time had surely come to call a halt to attempts to prove or disprove precognition. We should instead set about trying to harness and utilize it with a view to preventing future disasters." He began to work on a plan to set up a central clearing house where people might write or telephone if their psychic sense told them of future events of all kinds, including disasters. These would be computerized so that appropriate officials could be alerted.

The British Premonitions Bureau began operations in January, 1967. In its first year, information on about five hundred premonitions was received, among them four predictions of the assassination of Robert Kennedy. The predictions of several psychics who seemed to have an inborn sensitivity to future events were turned up among the thousand received up to May, 1970. The aims of the bureau have been redefined by the director who succeeded Dr. Barker after his sudden death in 1968 (he had forecast his own passing a year earlier), in these words: "Every effort is made to keep track of the events foretold and to retain an unbiased attitude toward the evidence. We neither believe nor disbelieve in premonitions as a possibility. We are simply curious."

The British Premonitions Bureau registers the premonitions it receives in various categories and has expanded its sphere of interest to other subjects besides natural disasters.

Early in 1968, Dr. Barker visited the United States and spoke about the formation of the British bureau at a meeting of the American Society for Psychical Research. The speech sparked the interest of Robert Nelson, a volunteer worker in the Maimonides Dream Laboratory, and he decided to establish a similar, but American, bureau in New York City. As a result, the Central Premonitions Registry came into being in June,

1968. Its purpose and structure were the same as the British bureau's, but contributors were expected to comply with two requirements: (1) Each premonition was to be recorded in writing and sent to the registry before the actual event, and it had to be sufficiently detailed and unusual enough to make coincidence unlikely. (2) If and when the event occurred, the person submitting the premonition had to send a newspaper clipping later that might validate the forecast. Premonitions of personal situations were not accepted, only items relating to public events and figures.

The categories first used by the registry were similar to those of the London bureau, with added files on subjects limited to the United States, such as the Kennedy family and other prominent Americans. In the first year of operation about six hundred premonitions were received, and as of early 1973, 3,500 predictions had been registered, but only about 1 percent of these have come true.

In addition to those received directly, the registry maintains a file of the predictions of such famous psychics as Jeane Dixon.

The progress of the registry thus far has been satisfactory. According to Mr. Nelson:

> Most of the people who write to us are ordinary individuals who are puzzled by their strange dreams. Their family and friends pay little attention to their premonitions, regarding them as "kooks." Yet it is the scientific study of such people that may lead to significant breakthroughs in understanding the mystery of the precognition process. The majority of these amateur psychics have not yet learned how to separate a valid premonition from one that may be motivated by their fears or may be pure fantasy.

Several contributors, however, have proved to be excellent psychics.

One potential of the registry is that continuous analysis of the premonitions submitted may eventually lead to a further accomplishment: the alerting of individuals and officials through a warning system.

Many parapsychologists feel that premonitory warnings should be carefully studied. Before the establishment of the two centers, Mrs. Louisa Rhine wrote in 1961 that "if imperfect ESP impressions, especially those suggesting disaster ahead, could be clarified, intelligent preventive action could follow to the untold advantage of mankind."

The opposite of precognition, advance knowledge of future events, is retrocognition, defined as "direct knowledge of the past without normal means." The term was invented by the pioneer British psychical researcher, F. W. H. Myers, who was also the first to use the word "telepathy." He defined retrocognition as "knowledge of the past supernormally acquired, that is, not gained through the senses from records or from the memory of living persons." The term generally refers to experiences in which an individual appears to be consciously or physically present in a bygone scene, perceiving it by sight and/or hearing, occasionally even by smell or touch.

The term cannot be found in dictionaries, and in the few psychic encyclopedias the word is usually defined as "the extrasensory perception of the past." A mere half dozen of the books examined by the author included the subject. However, retrocognition has been studied by a few investigators who have reported their findings in the *Journal* of the Society for Psychical Research (England) and the *Journal* and *Proceedings* of the American Society for Psychical Research.

The only full-length book on the subject is *Psychic Visits to the Past,* by Mrs. Gracia Fay Ellwood, a California author, published as a paperback original in 1971, which includes accounts of occurrences ranging in date from 1642 to 1963.

Mrs. Ellwood describes and illustrates three types of retrocognition. The most common is perception of a scene from the past, associated with a particular place, which she calls "walk-in retrocognition," because the individual seems to be physically present in the situation. For example, she recounts experiences of ten persons in 1901, 1902, 1908, 1928, and 1955, who were apparently "present" at Versailles while King Louis XV, Madame du Barry, his mistress, and Dauphine Marie Antoinette were living there. Most of the cases in the book are of this type.

Mrs. Ellwood's second category is "former incarnation," where, either in a trance or a waking state, a person describes a previous lifetime, giving a different name and identity, often seeming to become the other person altogether, believing himself to be in the midst of earlier circumstances. Mrs. Ellwood presents one such case.

In the third type, extraordinary knowledge of the past is associated with objects, and is a type of backward-looking psychometry or object reading. (As a form of clairvoyance, psychometry usually deals with current situations; see Chapter 6.) A psychically gifted person or sensitive will take an object with a rich history, perhaps holding it to his forehead. Information about the pasts of people who have touched it may come to him or he may see visions. One case is included in the book.

The question of historical collaboration is a very important one. Retrocognition can never be established as solidly as precognition, since the latter can be proved if and when the event involved takes place. For an apparently retrocognitive experience to be confirmed at all, according to Mrs. Ellwood, records must exist of the original event and/or people who remember it must still be available to give evidence. The possibility always exists that a person once heard or saw an account which, though he forgot it, remained in his unconscious.

The evidence for retrocognition is scanty, primarily due to the difficulty in ruling out telepathy or clairvoyance as alternative sources of information. This fascinating subject will undoubtedly continue to attract psychic investigators.

Often erroneously associated with retrocognition is *déjà vu* ("already seen"), which is defined as "the illusion of having experienced something actually being encountered for the first time." Within the past few decades, as ESP has been increasingly studied, however, parapsychologists have eliminated the *psi* factor in such experiences. Psychiatrists explain this phenomenon as a matter of "opening a false memory door," usually in dreams, wherein reality becomes vague and undefined. Sigmund Freud, the founder of psychoanalysis, termed it "a repudiation of reality."

Déjà vu may be a reincarnation memory. According

to Hans Holzer, it is "a feeling of having heard certain words spoken before in exactly the same manner as one now hears, or having been to a place before, where consciously and logically one knows one has never been."

Therefore, *déjà vu* is currently regarded as grounds for psychological rather than parapsychological study, and is not generally included in books on ESP.

CHAPTER 8

Psychokinesis

Were you to have consulted a dictionary for this word or sought information on it in an encyclopedia before 1940, you would not have found it. The dictionary, however, would have listed its two component parts: "psycho," mind, and "kinesis," movement or motion, both originating from Greek words. Their combination into a single new word introduced the world to a subdivision of parapsychology.

Current dictionary definitions of psychokinesis indicate its meaning. "The production of motion, especially in inanimate and remote objects, by the exercise of psychic powers" is one. "The mental power that moves objects or alters matter without physical contact" is another.

The Duke University parapsychologists defined it as "direct mental operation on a material body which produces a physical effect." They identified it simply as PK, and noted that it was the same as the familiar concept of mind over matter.

The idea of "mind over matter" is not new. Mediums, for instance, have often claimed an ability to influence objects in some unknown way, and have impressed the credulous by making tables and other articles rise in the air. Unfortunately such effects can easily be faked. In fact, that is the subject of Gian-Carlo Menotti's well-known and often-performed opera *The Medium.* The existence of fraud, however, does not give sufficient grounds for concluding that genuine mediums cannot produce the phenomenon of psychokinesis.

Psychokinesis differs from extrasensory perception, and the relation between them is still only partially understood. The view that has gained widest acceptance is that the two operations do involve essentially the same sort of interaction between the mind and the physical world.

Experimentation in psychokinesis at Duke University began in 1934. It came after the successes in telepathy, clairvoyance, and precognition, and was a logical follow-up to the ESP work. Dr. Rhine explained the link between them:

> In the clairvoyant perception of objects there has to be some operation between the mind and the material objects. Each must have an effect on the other. . . . The mind, therefore, does something to the object even though that something is too slight to be observed. The clairvoyance test was not designed to discover any such effect; what was needed was a means of measurement sensitive enough to register any such mental effect on the physical object.

Moving targets seemed to be the best place to start. After all, plenty of people think they can influence rolling dice or an arrow in flight by a direct action of the will, even if they don't believe they can make a stationary body move. Already the experimenters were conducting a kind of contest with chance by using guessing cards in the ESP test.

In the new tests dice served as the moving physical object. The various ESP controls were adapted to go with the new experiments. The recording of throw scores was simple, and the average for chance proved to be the same as for the cards.

After hundreds of tests with different objectives—throwing for each of the six faces and for specific combinations of the faces—the presence of *psi* was established. Since then, individual researchers elsewhere have made follow-up studies.

So-called spontaneous (nonlaboratory) cases of psychokinesis are practically unknown. Before PK became a study at Duke, a few cases had been reported to the various psychical research organizations but had been dismissed as being explained only in terms of "some unknown psychic power." At that time they could hardly be typed as psychokinesis, because the term had not yet been invented.

Dr. Rhine personally knew of very few occurrences before he undertook his experimental work. One that he included in *The Reach of the Mind* will show how almost unbelievable such cases may be. It concerned a college professor who taught courses in a department of religion:

> One day when he was discussing the question of immortality with a student, and just after he had been asked if he had ever

had any conclusive evidence of a spirit world, there came a sharp report. The student was really frightened. A heavy glass inkwell on the professor's desk was split clean into two pieces. The professor himself took the occurrence to be an effect of a nonphysical force of some kind, probably connected with a spirit. Certainly the case proves nothing, for we know that glass does break spontaneously, and this may have been mere coincidence.

An Ohio man reported the following experience to the Parapsychology Laboratory:

One Saturday afternoon I was sitting at my desk reading. Suddenly I felt a surge of blood racing through my veins; and at that same instant a picture of a close friend, hanging on the wall above my desk, dashed to the floor, breaking the glass but not injuring the photograph. Even before picking up the picture, I sat down at my typewriter and wrote to the friend. He lived about seven hundred miles away.

In due time I received a reply giving the address of a hospital. It seems that at the precise instant when the picture fell and I felt the sudden increase in blood pressure, my friend was driving in his car across a railroad track and was struck by a locomotive.

I was living in Cincinnati and he in New York state. He was recuperating from the accident when he replied to my letter.

The picture had been hanging there for six or eight months, and it was the string that broke. The picture was in an 8 × 10 wooden frame, and there was no heavy traffic or other jarring or vibration that could have caused it to fall. It fell without warning.

The poltergeist has only recently been accepted as a form of psychokinesis. Though many spontaneous cases have been documented and published, there has been a general unwillingness to believe such accounts.

The word "poltergeist" has a German origin. The Germans were the first to record such cases, starting as far back as 858. It means a noise-making or rattling (*poltern*) spirit (*Geist*).

A poltergeist causes a series of physical disturbances, such as noises (raps, scratching and sawing sounds, etc.) and movements of objects (kitchenware, tableware, furniture). The movements vary in kind and force. An object may fall to the floor, or it may be hurled some distance. Fragile items, of course, are broken, but no one is ever hit or hurt.

The disturbances take place most frequently in homes, but they may occur indoors in almost any building. They start unexpectedly and continue for an indefinite period of time, varying in duration from a few hours to weeks or months. The events tend to center around a particular person, usually someone who is young. The presence of this so-called "focal" person seems necessary for the disturbances to take place; strangely enough, this person must be awake.

Poltergeists are sometimes confused with hauntings. The word "haunt" comes from the same root as "home" and implies the belief that a spirit of a deceased person has remained at or returned to his earthly habitat. As a rule, hauntings do not seem to depend upon any particular living person but take place in a special locality such as a "haunted house."

Physical disturbances never occur in hauntings. Ghosts or spirits are silent, and they involve hallucinations, like "seeing ghosts" and "hearing footsteps," which are always in the mind of the person being haunted. Hauntings tend to last longer than poltergeist cases. It is not unusual to hear of a house that has been "haunted" for several years, but a poltergeist disturbance is usually of short duration and rarely lasts more than two months and often less.

As the name suggests, poltergeists were once considered to be evil or unhappy spirits. But because they usually occur in close proximity to a living ("focal") person, parapsychologists tend to regard them as instances of psychokinesis. From this standpoint, according to Dr. Joseph Pratt, the main question for investigation is: Did the focal person produce the events by trickery, either consciously or unconsciously? If not, an investigation may be directed toward a parapsychological explanation via PK.

Until the publication of a study of a 1958 case in Seaford, Long Island, no poltergeist case had ever appeared in any of the parapsychology journals during the preceding twenty-five years.

Though other cases had been reported throughout the world, the Seaford disturbances were the first in the United States to be investigated by serious researchers, in this case Drs. William Roll and J. Gaither Pratt of the Duke Parapsychology Laboratory, and they attracted national attention. The two professors later published a report in the *Journal of Parapsychology.*

On February 3, 1958, Mrs. James Herrmann and her children, aged twelve and thirteen, heard noises of bottles popping their caps and, checking, found that a bottle of holy water on her dresser had its cap unscrewed and was lying on its side with the contents spilled. In the son's adjoining bedroom, a small ceramic doll had its legs broken and a few small pieces had broken off a plastic ship model. In the bathroom cabinet two bottle caps were unscrewed and the contents spilled. In the kitchen Mrs. Herrmann found a bottle of starch under the sink with the cap off and contents running out. In the cellar directly under the kitchen a gallon of bleach was also uncapped and the contents drained out. There were other spillings on the sixth and seventh when the children were alone in the house.

On February 9, noises were heard coming in succession from different rooms. Spillings occurred again in the master bedroom, the bathroom, kitchen, and cellar while the family was at home and together in the dining room. The local police were then called, and when a patrolman arrived and was listening to the accounts, noises were heard in the bathroom, and he found that medicine and shampoo bottles had again spilled over.

When Dr. Rhine read of these occurrences in newspapers, he contacted the Herrmanns and the Seaford police. What he heard convinced him and other members of the Duke Laboratory staff that the cases were worth looking into. Before his assistants began their inquiry five weeks later, on March 10, a total of sixty-seven individual incidents had taken place. Members of the family watched bottles being moved and overturned, and a porcelain figurine on an end table next to a couch where a relative was sitting began to "wiggle" and then flew two feet into the room and landed on a rug with a loud, crashing sound, but it was not broken. This figurine later crashed to the floor three times without breaking, until it hit a desk standing ten feet away, marring the wood and breaking into bits.

A globe of the world in the son's room crashed to the floor three times, and a bottle of ink popped, became unscrewed, and landed about fifteen feet away in the next room, spilling on a chair, floor, and the wallpaper. While Mrs. Herrmann and the children were waiting in the front hall for the police to arrive, a loud noise was heard in the adjoining living room. A second figurine had left the end table and flown through the air for about ten feet and hit a desk, which broke it.

On the night of their arrival on March 10, the two Duke parapsychologists were listening to the accounts of the family members. There was a loud, dull noise from the cellar, and they found that a bleach bottle had lost its cap and fallen against the side of a utility box. This turned out to be the last performance of the Seaford poltergeist!

During the subsequent ten days, the investigators studied all phases of the disturbances. Of the sixty-seven incidents, three were unexplained thumping sounds and the rest movements of objects. A prominent feature was that the same article was often repeatedly involved. Sixteen separate objects were disturbed from two to four times each. The figurines in the living room moved six times before finally breaking. The Herrmann poltergeist seemed to like bottles; there were twenty-three "bottle poppings," more than a third of the occurrences. The bottles would lose their screw tops with an explosive sound, fall over, and spill their contents. Lamps and plates moved, and six pieces of furniture—bookcases, night tables, dressers, and a coffee table—were toppled over.

The Duke investigators determined that the occurrences could not have been due to radio or television waves or the electrical system. One of the most interesting revelations was that the poltergeist was active mainly when the twelve-year-old son Jimmy was in the house, a fact which corroborated the findings in other cases that children are almost always the focus of such disturbances.

The usual poltergeist has a reputation of being elusive. This was not true in Seaford; things happened when the police and outside visitors were present.

Subsequently, in the 1960s, about fifty poltergeist cases were known to have occurred in the United States, and many were reported upon, several by Pratt and Roll. The investigations of poltergeist phenomena thus became a recognized part of parapsychology.

Many people feel that the poltergeist phenomenon is one that scientists should not consider. To them the study of spirits and ghosts seems to be ridiculous. Yet, as Dr. Pratt explains, "here we are once again with yet another kind of unexplained natural occurrence that appears to signal an event in some corners of the universe on which men has only recently turned his powerful searchlight of . . . inquiry. . . . We must admit that among the difficult questions encountered in parapsychology, the poltergeist is one of the hardest of all."

A form of psychokinesis which is currently attracting considerable attention is psychic photography, or the ability to imprint mental images on photographic film by no normal means. This is called Kirlian photography after its discoverer, a Russian electrician named Semyon Kirlian, and shows an aura which changes according to good or bad health. The subject is discussed in Chapter 9.

CHAPTER 9

New Frontiers in Parapsychology

Mental healing is as old as man. In primitive tribes there was often a medicine man or witch doctor with the ability to heal. This power was thought to be magic. Characterized as faith healing, it later became related to religion, and bodily ills were treated not with medicines but through some spiritual attitude on the part of the sufferer. The priest became the medium through which healing was accomplished.

In his "miracle" healings, Jesus relied on the power of suggestion. "Take up your bed and walk," he said. He declared that God provided the healing force and that a sick person could tap it through him or his disciples: "Thy faith hath made thee whole."

Psychic healing involves the "laying on of hands" by a person acting as a medium between the ailing individual and his mind. This ability to stop or reverse the progress of disease is recognized by many doctors, who realize how much thought and attitude affect the condition of their patients. Religious healers continuously exhibit their power with what *Newsweek* has termed "doses of faith and hope, with a mystery ingredient."

The latter phrase indicates the parapsychological element; it is "psychic energy."

One of the things that greatly spurred research in this phenomenon was the sudden interest in acupuncture that arose when distinguished American doctors visited China in the early 1970s. Acupuncture theory stresses that there is an energy system interpenetrating the body, through which the energy, *ch'i*, flows. The acupuncturists believe that this energy system, even though invisible, is just as important to the body as the circulatory or nervous system.

Additional evidence of the existence of psychic energy was unfolded when Dr. Bernard Grad of McGill University conducted tests in 1960 on Oskar Estebany, a former Hungarian army officer living in Canada, who claimed to have a special healing power in his hands. Experimenting with laboratory mice who had superficial wounds, Grad found that healing occurred faster when Estebany brought his hands near the cage and held them there than it did when another person not claiming healing power held his hands there.

New York psychologist Lawrence LeShan, a pioneer in the study of psychic healing, asserts:

> What we are seeing is the turn of American medicine to the concept that healing involves the whole person. We are learning that the psychic attitude of physicians and nurses can affect the physical rehabilitation of a patient in their care. And physicians themselves are discovering a whole person who is involved in the healing process.

In his *The Medium, the Mystic, and the Physicist* (1974),

LeShan argues that most psychic healing is actually accomplished by the patient's own "self-healing mechanisms which have been mobilized by the healer." The healer sets the mechanism in motion through an exercise of consciousness that unites him with the patient. "In this fashion," LeShan maintains, "arthritis, bursitis and other ailments can sometimes be healed, and even some supposedly terminal cancerous tumors can be controlled.

"Such healings look miraculous," he admits, "but that is only because we ordinarily operate far below our psychic potentialities."

In an attempt to refine and test his theories, LeShan has trained more than 150 healers, but he reports that only about 10 percent of the cases studied can be "classified as unquestionably valid and unattributable to any other causes."

Among others, ex-astronaut Edgar Mitchell is particularly interested in "the humanitarian aspects" of psychic healing, and his Institute of Noetic Sciences is conducting investigations. Admitting that he does not know where the energy comes from, he has stated, "Conscious energy seems to have a universal nature; it is just as real as any of the other energies science has tried to understand."

Many psychic healers are operating today, but they are not recognized, of course, by the American Medical Association. Therefore, psychic healing is illegal in the United States except when money does not change hands.

A type of healing related to the psychic but not recognized as a part of it is "divine healing." In such cases, the healing is believed to be supernatural, and the medium acts only as an agent between the patient and God. Kathryn Kuhlman and Oral Roberts are the best known of such healers.

One aspect of healing is the use of so-called psychic surgery wherein individuals who have no medical training or knowledge of modern sanitation perform operations without using any instruments. Diagnosing illnesses and locating diseased organs by purely psychic means, they plunge their hands through what appear to be deep incisions (without using scalpels) to grasp and remove diseased tissues. The Philippines is currently the center for such work.

The best-known Filipino surgeon is Antonio Agpaoa, though he is more commonly known as "Dr. Tony." Ian Stevenson, who visited him several times, gave a detailed report at the 1966 convention of the Parapsychology Association. According to him, Agpaoa and his colleagues operated within the framework of spiritualism. They made incisions, opened the abdominal cavity, and removed tissues without knives, with no infection, with little or no bleeding, and with very rapid healing of the wounds or openings.

After a visit the next year, Harold Sherman wrote a book about them titled *"Wonder" Healers of the Philippines* (1967). Mr. Sherman was critical of the "doctors" and their methods, since he detected some fraud and trickery. (It is thought in some circles that the organs "removed" from patients are animal organs skillfully palmed by sleight of hand.) However, Mr. Sherman was personally convinced that genuine psychic "surgery" does sometimes take place. A prime example of the latter is Tony Roche, a tennis star, who was relieved of painful "tennis elbow" when three blood clots were apparently removed by the touch of a healer in the Philippines.

In a backwoods mining town in Brazil, the late José Arigo performed hundreds of "operations" on peasants using only a penknife. His work is described in John Fuller's *Arigo: Surgeon of the Rusty Knife*, published in 1974. Fifteen American doctors under Dr. Andrija Puharich spent a week investigating Arigo's methods and were able to report only that they remained "mystified as to how he operates." Dr. Puharich himself underwent an operation by Arigo for the extraction of an arm tumor. Such an operation usually takes at least fifteen minutes. Arigo performed it in fifteen seconds! Afterward Dr. Puharich said, "The mystery is not in the absence of anesthesia but in the whole surgical process employed by Arigo. Some of his diagnoses would normally be possible only by X-rays."

Research in psychic healing has recently stimulated enormous interest in a technique called Kirlian photography. In this process, named after the Russian husband-and-wife team who developed it in 1939, the object to be photographed, usually a human finger, is placed on photographic film, while a faint electric current passes between the finger and the film. When the film is developed it shows colorful, wavy patterns surrounding the tip of the finger, much as an X-ray would reveal the inner structure. Tests show that the patterns vary with the subject's emotional and physical state and could be used to diagnose disease.

Kirlian photography has led to numerous energy-related theories for explaining the whole range of pyschic phenomena. The Russians have labeled the energy field bio-plasma, but except for an account in Ostrander and Schroeder's *Psychic Discoveries Behind the Iron Curtain* few details of their work have been released. Dr. Douglas Dean, an electrochemist who conducts experiments at the Newark (New Jersey) College of Engineering, speculates that the energy waves are of very low frequency and travel faster than light, a feat some physicists claim is possible.

Both Dr. Dean and Dr. Thelma Moss of the University of California at Los Angeles' Neuropsychiatric Institute have claimed that Kirlian photographs show psychic healers to have a smaller glow after healing than before, while their patients emit brighter glows.

Dr. Moss, who has taken more Kirlian photographs and done more experimental work than anyone outside of Russia, believes that Kirlian photography clearly demonstrates the existence of a human aura. "We at UCLA have done work with acupuncturists and psychic healers," she says, "and we find that the corona of the healer becomes intense before healing and then afterward is more relaxed and less strong. We think we're looking at a transfer of energy from the healer to the injured person."

Others are less certain. Writing in the Photographic Society of America's *Journal,* Bill Zalud concluded, "All speculation hinges on obtaining normal tissue patterns for comparative purposes and, so far, no one has really determined what a normal Kirlian photograph is." And Professor William Tiller of Stanford University has pointed out, "Most of the effects actually have non-psychic explanations. But for just that reason, Kirlian photography could become an important research and diagnostic tool." The pros and cons will undoubtedly continue to be debated.

The most controversial figure in Kirlian photography in the United States during the 1960s was Ted Serios, whose demonstrations of his apparent ability to create pictures of his thoughts on Polaroid film made him a television star. He produced his pictures inside a Polaroid camera by using, as he says, "nothing but my mind and a paper tube called a 'gismo.' "

No serious investigators monitored his achievements until Drs. J. Gaither Pratt and Ian Stevenson conducted a series of forty-six trials in 1967 at the University of Virginia. Though all the prints had apparently been produced parapsychologically, they formed no final opinion because he always used his tube of rolled-up paper and appeared to be dependent upon it. The question in their minds was whether an element of trickery had been involved.

In several thousand other trials which produced more than a thousand paranormal pictures under persons trained in both science and stage magic—the latter to determine whether the success was due to trickery—the photographs appeared to be genuine. Two writers for *Popular Photography* magazine observed Serios at work in

Denver in 1968, and in a published article they made strong imputation of fraud on the basis of what they had seen. In further trials with Pratt and Stevenson, Serios failed to produce valuable and clear pictures. For that reason, his successes are still being questioned, and until other individuals with PK abilities turn up, Kirlian photography will continue to be controversial.

However, this work with Serios resulted in a serious bid for the attention of other parapsychologists, but other unsuccessful periods have lasted about two years, and he has not yet continued his demonstrations. The future of this fascinating line of investigation will depend upon the availability for study of other persons with similar abilities.

In the fall of 1973 a book called *The Secret Life of Plants,* by Peter Tompkins and Christopher Bird, was published with little fanfare and advance publicity. But as sometimes happens in the publishing business, it caught on even before reviews appeared in late November and December. In the book trade it became what is termed "a sleeper," even though the reviews varied from favorable to bad, with some of them hostile and maliciously derogatory. Even so, the book soon reached the national best seller list, where it remained among the ten top nonfiction titles throughout the early months of 1974, and its popularity with the public appears to be durable.

The thesis of the book is that plants can sense the thoughts of human beings. Citing scores of experiments and the testimony of hundreds of plant lovers who possess "green thumbs," the authors let growers, professional and amateur, describe their own observations of plants' reactions to music, people, electromagnetism, organic gardening, and their environment.

Plant lovers have long recognized that plants respond to loving care and the atmosphere surrounding them. When he was developing his new varieties, Luther Burbank admitted that he "created a vibration of love" for them.

During the 1950s, while the Reverend Franklin Loehr was minister of the First Congregational Church of Los Angeles, he conducted seven hundred experiments with more than 150 persons, using more than 27,000 seeds and seedlings, researching into the effect of prayer on plants. The results, published in a 1959 book, appear to prove that the seeds that received prayer treatment grew more rapidly than the control group of seeds that were ignored.

At McGill University, Dr. Bernard Grad, who experimented with Oskar Estebany on healing (see above), made tests with him on plantings of barley seeds. Estebany simply held his hands near them, without contact, while other similar plantings were left untreated. Again the results were successful: Better germination and more rapid early growth occurred in the treated barley than in the untreated plantings. In still another test Estebany held his hands near closed bottles of water that would later be used to water plantings of barley, while other bottles of water to be used on other similar plantings were left untreated. Those seeds watered from the bottles "treated" by Estebany germinated and grew significantly better than did those watered from the untreated bottles.

In a further stage of testing, the possibility of Estebany's influencing the rate of growth of molds was investigated. In this instance, as in the previous ones, the claim for a special healing power was supported by the laboratory findings. Subsequently, Estebany was also studied by an investigator in another laboratory, and the results were reported at the 1968 convention of the Parapsychology Association. They conformed with those obtained earlier by Dr. Grad.

Many experiments have indicated that plants, like human beings, have emotions. For example, Clyde Backster, a New York City lie-detector specialist, wanted to determine whether a plant, a philodendron in the experiment, reacts to being watered. In various books and articles, he has told how his experiment was carried out. A pair of electrodes connected to a recording instrument were attached to a leaf with a rubber band. Backster had expected to see a steady downward line on the chart as the plant absorbed moisture. Instead the line gradually went upward, making occasional jumps just the way a human heart does when short emotional action is being measured.

That made Backster wonder what would happen if he made a threat to the plants, similar to the loaded-question technique of triggering emotional responses in people on lie-detector tests. He decided to light a match to the hooked-up leaf. The moment he made this conscious decision—before he even touched the plant or made a move to get a match—the stress line on the polygraph zoomed upward. The philodendron had seemingly read his mind!

The Kirlian photography process has produced some very strange pictures of plants. Multicolored lights shine from them like a "luminous coat of arms," identifying each species. In experiments in both Russia and Los Angeles leaves have been cut in half and photographed. The pictures miraculously show the "aura" or outline of the whole leaf. One can see what seem like rays of energy shooting out of the plants.

Russian scientists photographed a lilac stem with two buds. In the first picture they saw plumes of light pouring out of the buds and small spikes of light like a luminous crown. Then they cut each bud in half. The radiant spikes still showed, this time even clearer. They lopped off the buds completely, and great beams of energy shot from the end of the stem like a Roman candle.

Though these experiences may be difficult to accept, they definitely indicate that *psi* exists in plants.

CHAPTER 10

The Future

The new study of parapsychology began with the accumulated interest that was aroused by an increasing number of reports of human experiences and events known as psychic. These puzzling phenomena had never been claimed or accepted by any of the established branches of science, and until the 1930s all but a few scientists had ignored their existence. Parapsychology was the result of a desire on the part of nineteenth-century scholars to find out whether all nature was purely physical. The question was: "Are there mental processes that are not part of the material world?" In their search for an answer to this question the founders of parapsychology were looking for nonphysical (mental) phenomena in nature that might be scientifically observed and described.

Louisa Rhine has stated the problem in these words:

> What is man? Is he a creation of "sense and mechanics" only, or something more? . . . Increasingly, as fields of physics, chemistry, and mechanics have developed, the impression has deepened that human beings are, to put it simply, just machines. Very complicated machines, of course, but still

> essentially mechanisms. Already many known laws of matter, body, and mind suggest it.
>
> The great developments of which this age is proud, however, were not brought about by guesses, beliefs, or assumptions. They are the results of the careful, controlled methods of experimental science. Certainly the same reliable objective methods should be demanded for research on the elemental question of man's own nature.

As noted in Chapter 4, many scientists and laymen are still antagonistic toward the new study. Their criticisms, of course, have been based on the validity of the tests. All of the techniques used had to be specially designed, and the critics have wondered whether the interpretations and evaluations of the results have been statistically sound.

All the same, parapsychology has withstood all attacks and is gaining in approval and recognition. As interest in the subject increases, ever-new aspects of it are being investigated, with the hope that we can expand our knowledge of *psi* power.

However, many people still confuse parapsychology with occultism, and authors persist in including the latter in their writings, as if by adding them to the parapsychology bandwagon, they will give credence to such activities.

One of the characteristics of this study of the mind has been the readiness of researchers to widen the scope of their investigations. This extension in fields of interest has been particularly evident since 1960. Initial work has begun in the following fields of inquiry in the United States: survival after death, the validity of mediums, reincarnation, and astral projection.

Survival after death is being studied by the Psychical Research Foundation, established in 1960 at Durham, North Carolina. Under the terms of the charter, its research must be directed specifically toward "investigations bearing upon the question of whether any part or aspect of human personality survives death." Under the direction of William G. Roll, who had worked with Rhine and Pratt at Duke University, special phases of spiritualism are beginning to be examined for evidences of *psi* power.

During the second half of the nineteenth century and into the present one, before parapsychology appeared on the scene, psychic researchers investigated a great many mediums, exposing charlatans and frauds. It is difficult to determine whether a medium in a trance produces information telepathically from the sitter or gets it from other sources by means of clairvoyance. This and the role of automatic writing in séances as a form of spirit manifestation have yet to be explained.

Reincarnation is the belief that each individual person possesses an element, independent of his physical being, which after his death can be reborn into another body. The idea of reincarnation is probably as old as religion itself, for it has been around since the beginning of civilization. One of the problems in proving reincarnation is that very few people are able, under normal circumstances, to remember their previous lives.

Dr. Ian Stevenson, who has become a leader in the revival of interest in survival, has spent several years investigating man's dream of immortality through reincarnation. He studied hundreds of reports from people all over the world who claim to recall a previous life.

His *Twenty Cases Suggestive of Reincarnation,* published by the American Society for Psychical Research in 1966, examined twenty cases in detail. Though he has continued his studies, the evidence is still in question, but reincarnation remains a legitimate subject for parapsychological study.

Out-of-body projection, formerly called astral projecting or astral travel, is the experience of leaving the body and traveling in the atmosphere. Generally, the astral body rises horizontally about three feet above the physical body before beginning its journey. The traveler is able to give an accurate account of his experience later. Many cases have been reported, but as yet only one serious study, *Journeys Out of Body* (1971) by Robert Monroe, has been made of this phenomenon. An objective, controlled type of study is needed. The most active current investigator is Dr. Chárles T. Tart of the University of California at Davis, who has great hopes that his findings will aid in an understanding of this phenomenon.

The various phases of psychic phenomena continue to have a fascination for the public and for those who do research in this comparatively new field of study. Prospects for further additions to present knowledge in many areas are boundless. What Mrs. Louisa Rhine called the "reaches of the mind" are proving to be almost limitless.

ESP Tests

The discovery and uses of ESP are discussed in two popularly written books, both available in paperback:

Sherman, Harold, *How to Make ESP Work for You.* New York, Crest (paperback), 1964.
Smith, Susy, *How to Develop Your ESP.* New York, Putnam, 1972. Paperback: Pinnacle Books.

The following items will be useful in such a determination:

ESP cards: The deck of the official ESP (Zener) cards, with procedures for testing and scoring, developed in the Duke University Parapsychology Laboratory, are available from the Foundation for Research on the Nature of Man, Box 6846, College Station, Durham, N. C. 27708, for $1.50. Record sheets 50 for 50 cents. Also Louisa F. Rhine's *Manual for Introductory Experiments in Parapsychology* (1966), for $1.

Card decks are also available in some bookstores or from Haines House of Cards, Norwood, Ohio 45212. $1.50.

Books and Periodical Articles:

Cope, Lloyd A., *Develop Your ESP.* New York, Dell Parse Books (paperback), 1973.
Ebon, Martin, ed., *Test Your ESP.* New York, World, 1970. Paperback: Signet. Excerpts in *Ladies Home Journal*, Vol. 88 (May, 1971), p. 78.

Gardner, Martin, "Astounding Self-test of Clairvoyance by Dr. Matrix." *Scientific American*, Vol. 229 (August, 1973), pp. 98–101.

Holzer, Hans, *The Handbook of Parapsychology*. Los Angeles, Nash Publishing Co., 1971, pp. 167–69.

Hoy, David, *Psychic and Other ESP Party Games*. Garden City, N. Y., Doubleday, 1965. Paperback: Funk and Wagnalls.

Logan, Daniel, *Do You Have ESP? Thirty Tests to Determine Your Ability*. Garden City, N. Y., Doubleday, 1970.

Mademoiselle, Vol. 73 (June, 1971), pp.138–39. Includes tests for clairvoyance, dowsing, and plant growing.

McConnell, Robert A., *ESP Curriculum Guide*. New York, Simon and Schuster, 1971. Paperback: Fireside Books. Tests of picture drawing and card guessing, pp. 95–110.

Rhine, Joseph Banks, "A New Case of Experimenter Unreliability," *Journal of Parapsychology*, Vol. 38 (June, 1974).

——— "Security Versus Deception in Parapsychology," *Journal of Parapsychology*, Vol. 38 (March, 1974).

An *ESP Portfolio* which includes information sheets and reprints of selected articles from various journals, and three game tests for telepathy and clairvoyance using the Zener cards and pictures, may be obtained from the American Society for Psychical Research, 5 West 73rd Street, New York, N. Y. 10023. Price $3 plus 50 cents for postage and handling. The Zener cards may also be purchased ($1.50).

Organizations

American Society for Psychical Research, 5 West 73d Street, New York, N. Y., 10023.

Foundation for Research on the Nature of Man, Box 6846, College Station, Durham, N. C. 27708.

Parapsychological Association, Care Dr. J. G. Pratt, Box 152, University of Virginia Hospital, Charlottesville, Va. 22901.

Parapsychology Foundation, Inc., 29 West 57th Street, New York, N. Y. 10019.

Selected Sources and Readings

The literature of parapsychology is extensive and, because of the current popular interest, is increasing. The criterion in selection is availability; hence some of the out-of-print standard books are not included unless they have been reprinted or have been issued in paperback editions. Others have been omitted because they may be obtained in only the largest library collections. Most of the titles listed under "books" include bibliographies. The life of paperback editions is often short, and they become out-of-print rapidly. A notable trend, however, is the publication of originals in this form. Many of the popularly written books and original paperbacks on ESP, however, include subjects which have not yet been accepted as possessing evidence of *psi* (see Chapter 10), as well as the occult fields which are not relevant to parapsychology.

Starred (*) titles are recommended for beginners and high-school students.

Bibliographies

White, Rhea, "Parapsychology Books on Campus." *Psychic*, Vol. 5 (November–December, 1973), pp. 23–27. Annotated general list for college courses.

——— "Resources in the Field: Parapsychology: The Psychic World." *Wilson Library Bulletin*, Vol. 47 (November, 1972), pp. 262–74. Annotated list for libraries.

*——— and Dale, Laura A., eds., *Parapsychology: Sources of Information*. Metuchen, N. J., Scarecrow Press, 1973. An all-inclusive list of books on all phases of parapsychology. Lengthy descriptive

annotations analyze the coverage, cite reviews, and include reading level.

Study and Research

Ashby, Robert H., *The Guidebook for the Study of Psychical Research.* New York, Samuel Weiser, Inc., 1972.

McConnell, Robert A., *ESP Curriculum Guide.* New York, Simon and Schuster, 1971. Paperback: Fireside Books.

Books

Agee, Doris, *Edgar Cayce on ESP.* New York, Paperback Library (paperback), 1969.

Angoff, Allan, ed., *Psychic Force: Excursions in Parapsychology.* New York, Putnam, 1970.

——— and Shapin, Betty, eds., *A Century of Psychical Research: The Continuing Doubts and Affirmations.* New York, Parapsychology Foundation, 1971.

——— *Parapsychology Today: A Geographic View.* New York, Parapsychology Foundation, 1973.

Archer, Fred, *Crime and the Psychic World.* New York, Morrow, 1969.

Bridge, Ann (pseud.), *Moments of Knowing: Personal Experiences in the Realm of Extra-Sensory Perception.* New York, McGraw-Hill, 1970.

Cavendish, Richard, ed., *The Encyclopedia of the Unexplained: Magic, Occultism and Parapsychology.* New York, McGraw-Hill, 1974. Special consultant on parapsychology, J. B. Rhine.

Christopher, Milbourne, *ESP, Seers and Psychics.* New York, Crowell, 1970.

*Cohen, Daniel, *ESP: The Search Beyond the Senses.* New York, Harcourt Brace Jovanovich, 1973.

Ebon, Martin, ed., *The Psychic Reader.* New York, World, 1969. Paperback: Signet.

——— *The Psychic Scene.* New York, Signet (paperback), 1974.

*Edmonds, Simeon, *ESP: Extrasensory Perception.* North Hollywood, Calif., Wilshire Book Company (paperback), 1973.

Fodor, Nandor, ed., *Encyclopedia of Psychic Science.* New Hyde Park, N. Y., University Books, 1966. Paperback: Citadel Press.

*Greenhouse, Herbert B., *The Book of Psychic Knowledge: All Your Questions Answered.* New York, Taplinger, 1973.

Haynes, Renée, *The Hidden Springs: An Enquiry into Extra-Sensory Perception.* Rev. ed. Boston, Little Brown, 1973.

*Hyde, Margaret O., and others, *Mysteries of the Mind.* New York, McGraw-Hill, 1972. For teen-agers.

*Johnson, Raynor C., *Psychical Research: Exploring the Supernatural.* New York, Funk and Wagnalls, 1968. Paperback: Funk and Wagnalls.

*Kettelkamp, Larry, *Sixth Sense.* New York, Morrow, 1970. For grades 5–9.

*Klein, Aaron E., *Beyond Time and Matter: A Sensory Look at ESP.* Garden City, N. Y., Doubleday, 1973. For grades 8–12.

Koestler, Arthur, *The Roots of Coincidence: An Excursion into Parapsychology.* New York, Random House, 1972.

*MacKenzie, Andrew, *Frontiers of the Unknown: The Insights of Psychical Research.* London, Barker, 1968. Out of print. Paperback: Popular Library.

Mitchell, Edgar D., ed., *Psychic Exploration: A Challenge for Science.* New York, Putnam, 1974. Chapters on all phases of parapsychology by specialists.

Murphy, Gardner, and Dale, Laura A., *Challenge of Psychical Research: A Primer of Parapsychology.* New York, Harper and Row, 1961. Paperback: Colophon Books.

Neff, H. Richard, *Psychic Phenomena and Religion: ESP, Prayer, Healing, Survival.* Philadelphia, Westminster Press, 1971. Paperback: Westminster Press.

Ostrander, Sheila, and Schroeder, Lynn, *Handbook of Psi Discoveries.* New York, Putnam, 1974.

*Pratt, J. Gaither, *ESP Research Today.* Metuchen, N. J., Scarecrow Press, 1973.

*——— *Parapsychology: An Insider's View of ESP.* Rev. ed. New York, Dutton, 1966.

——— and others, *Extra-sensory Perception After Sixty Years.* (1940). Reprint: Boston, Branden Press, 1966.

Rhine, Joseph Banks, *Extra-sensory Perception.* (1934). Rev. ed. Boston, Branden Press, 1964. Out of print. Paperback: Branden Press.

——— *New Frontiers of the Mind: The Story of the Duke Experiments.* New York, Farrar and Rinehart, 1937. Out of print. Reprint: Greenwood Press.

——— *New World of the Mind.* New York, William Sloane Associates, 1937. Out of print. Paperback: Apollo Editions.

——— *The Reach of the Mind.* New York, Morrow, 1947. Out of print. Reprint: Peter Smith. Paperback: New York, Apollo Editions.

——— ed. *Progress in Parapsychology.* Durham, N. C., Parapsychology Press, 1971. Also in paperback.

——— and others, *Parapsychology from Duke to FRNM.* Paperback original: Durham, N. C., Parapsychology Press, 1965.

——— and Brier, Robert, ed., *Parapsychology Today.* New York, Citadel Press, 1968.

——— and Pratt, J. Gaither, *Parapsychology: Frontier Science of the Mind.* Rev. ed. Springfield, Ill., C. C. Thomas, 1962.

Rhine, Louisa E., *ESP in Life and Lab: Tracing Hidden Channels.* New York, Macmillan, 1967. Paperback: Collier-Macmillan.

——— *Hidden Channels of the Mind.* New York, William Sloane Associates, 1961. Out of print. Paperback: Apollo Editions.

Rose, Ronald, *Living Magic.* New York, Rand McNally, 1956. Out of print. A classic study.

Ryzl, Milan, *Parapsychology: A Scientific Approach.* New York, Hawthorn, 1970.

Schmiedler, Gertrude, ed., *Extrasensory Perception.* New York, Atherton, 1969. Paperback: Aldine Press.

*Sherman, Harold, *Your Mysterious Powers of ESP: The New Medium of Communication.* New York, World, 1969. Out-of-print. Paperback: Signet.

*Smith, Susy, *ESP.* New York, Pyramid Publications (paperback), 1972; Los Angeles, Sherbourne Press (paperback), 1972.

——— *ESP and Hypnosis.* New York, Macmillan, 1973.

——— *More ESP.* Los Angeles, Sherbourne Press (paperback), 1972.

*Somerlott, Robert, "*Here, Mr. Splitfoot*". New York, Viking, 1971.

Spraggett, Allen, *Probing the Unexplained.* New York, Signet (paperback), 1971.

——— *The Unexplained.* New York: Signet (paperback), 1962.

——— *The World of the Unexplained.* New York, Signet (paperback), 1974.

Van Over, Raymond, ed., *Psychology and Extrasensory Perception.* New York, Mentor (paperback), 1972.

Periodical Articles

For more technical treatments, the periodicals of research organizations, noted in Chapter 3, are valuable. Because they are generally unavailable in many libraries, only a few references to them are cited in this reading list.

"Boom Times on the Psychic Frontier." *Time*, Vol. 103 (March 4, 1974), pp. 65–72.

Chance, Paul, "Parapsychology Is an Idea Whose Time Has Come." *Psychology Today*, Vol. 7 (October, 1973), pp. 105–20.

Gray, Francine du Plessix, "Parapsychology and Beyond," *New York Times Magazine*, August 11, 1974.

Hughes, Robert, "Cosmos Is a Giant Thought." *Horizon*, Vol. 16 (Winter, 1973–74), pp. 4–21.

Marks, Jane, "ESP Is Never Having to Say You're Psychic." *Mademoiselle*, Vol. 73 (June, 1971), pp. 138–39.

"Parapsychology: The Science of the Uncanny." *Newsweek*, Vol. 83 (March 4, 1974), pp. 52–57.

Parapsychology in Russia

Agnew, Irene, "Parapsychology in Russia." *Science Digest*, Vol. 72 (July, 1972), pp. 69–71.

Krippner, Stanley, and Davidson, Richard, "Parapsychology in the U. S. S. R." *Saturday Review*, Vol. 55 (March 18, 1972), pp. 56–60.

Krippner, Stanley, and Hickman, James, "West Meets East." *Psychic*, Vol. 5 (May–June, 1974), pp. 51–55.

Ostrander, Sheila, and Schroeder, Lynn, *Psychic Discoveries Behind the Iron Curtain*. Englewood Cliffs, N. J., Prentice-Hall, 1970. Paperback: Bantam Books.

Biography

Asch, Robert H., "Important Figures in Psychical Research," *The Guidebook for the Study of Psychical Research*. New York, Samuel Weiser, Inc., 1972.

Garrett, Eileen, *Adventures in the Supernormal: A Personal Memoir*. New York, Garrett-Helix, 1949. Paperback: Paperback Library.

——— *Many Voices: The Autobiography of a Medium*. New York, Putnam, 1968.

Moss, Thelma, *Psychics, Saints and Scientists*. New York, Hawthorn,

1974.
*_Psychics_, by the editors of _Psychic_ magazine. New York, Harper Row, 1972. Note: A biography is included in each issue of _Psychic_.
*Smith, Eleanor T., _Psychic People_. New York, Morrow, 1968. Paperback: Bantam Books. Biographies of nineteen psychics.

Cayce, Edgar

Sugrue, Thomas, _There Is a River: The Story of Edgar Cayce_. Rev. ed. New York, Holt, Rinehart and Winston, 1966. Paperback: Dell.

Geller, Uri

Kiester, Edwin, Jr., "Behind Science's Growing Fascination with Psychic Phenomena: Feats of U. Geller." _Today's Health_, Vol. 51 (November, 1973), pp. 24–27.
"The Phenomenon of Uri Geller." _Psychic_, Vol. 4 (June, 1973), pp. 3–18.
Puharich, Andrija, _Uri: A Journal of the Mystery of Uri Geller_. Garden City, N. Y., Doubleday, 1974.
Weil, Andrew, "Uri Geller and Parapsychology." _Psychology Today_, Vol. 8, (June, 1974, pp. 45–50; July, 1974, pp. 74–78).

Hurkos, Peter

Browning, Norma Lee, _The Psychic World of Peter Hurkos_. Garden City, N. Y., Doubleday, 1970. Paperback: Signet.
Boston Strangler case: _Life_, Vol. 56 (March 6, 1964), pp. 49–50; _Newsweek_, Vol. 63 (February 24, 1964), p. 31.

Kreskin, George

Kreskin, George, _The Amazing World of Kreskin_. New York, Random House, 1973.

Casebooks

Occurrences are often described in _Fate Magazine_ and _The National Enquirer_.
*Ebon, Martin, _They Knew the Unknown_. New York, World, 1971.

Out of print. Paperback: Signet.

MacKenzie, Andrew, *The Unexplained: Some Strange Cases of Psychical Research.* New York, Abelard-Schuman, 1970. Paperback: Popular Library.

*Prince, Walter F., *Noted Witnesses for Psychic Occurrences.* New Hyde Park, N. Y., University Books, 1963. Paperback abridgement under title *They Saw Beyond: Distinguished Witnesses to Psychic Phenomena*: Olympia Press.

Science and ESP

*Cohen, Daniel, "ESP: Science or Delusion?" *Nation*, Vol. 202 (May 9, 1966), pp. 550–53.

*——— "Science Gets Serious About ESP." *Science Digest*, Vol. 58 (November, 1965), pp. 62–72.

Hansel, C. E. M., *ESP: A Scientific Evaluation.* New York, Scribner, 1966. Paperback: Lyceum Editions.

McBee, Susanna, "A Scientist Looks at ESP: Visit with J. Pratt at the University of Virginia." *McCall's*, Vol. 97 (March, 1970), pp. 50, 52, 141.

*Pierce, Henry W., *Science Looks at ESP.* New York, New American Library, 1970. Out of print. Paperback: Signet.

*Price, George R., "Science and the Supernatural." *Science*, Vol. 122 (August 26, 1955), pp. 359–67. Discussion in *Science*, Vol. 123 (January 6, 1956), pp. 9–19. Reply in *Science*, Vol. 175 (January 28, 1972), p. 359. Reprint: Indianapolis, Ind., Bobbs Merrill, 1973.

*Stevenson, Ian, "Uncomfortable Facts About ESP." *Harper's Magazine*, Vol. 219 (July, 1959), pp. 19–25.

Wade, Nicholas, "Psychical Research: The Incredible in Search of Credibility." *Science*, Vol. 181 (July 13, 1973), pp. 138–43. Discussion in *Science*, Vol. 182 (October 19, 1973), p. 222.

"Why Scientists Take Psychic Research Seriously." *Business Week*, January 26, 1974, pp. 76–78.

Animals and ESP

*Cohen, Daniel, *Talking with Animals.* New York, Dodd Mead, 1971.

Gaddis, Vincent and Margaret, *The Strange World of Animals and Pets*. New York, Cowles, 1970. Out of print. Paperback: Pocket Books.

Morris, Robert L., "Animals and ESP." *Psychic*, Vol. 5 (September-October, 1973), pp. 13–17.

Telepathy

*Garrett, Eileen, *Telepathy*. New York, Garrett Publications, 1968.

*Mitchell, Edgar D., "An ESP Test from Apollo 14." *Journal of Parapsychology*, Vol. 35 (June, 1971), pp. 89–107.

Schreiber, Flora R., and Herman, Melvin, "ESP Enters the Laboratory." *Science Digest*, Vol. 60 (October, 1966), pp. 48–54.

*Sinclair, Upton, *Mental Radio*. (c1930). 2d rev. ed. Springfield, Ill., C. C. Thomas, 1962. Paperback: Macmillan-Collier.

Soal, S. G., and Bateman, F., *Modern Experiments in Telepathy*. London, Faber and Faber, 1954. A classic study.

Stevenson, Ian, *Telepathic Impressions*. Charlottesville, Va., University of Virginia Press, 1970.

Tenhaeff, W. H. C., *Telepathy and Clairvoyance: Views on Some Little Investigated Capabilities of Man*. Springfield, Ill., C. C. Thomas, 1973.

Dreams

*Ford, Barbara, "ESP in the Dream Laboratory." *Science Digest*, Vol. 67 (January, 1970), pp. 10–18.

McBroom, Patricia, "Dreams, Art and Mental Telepathy." *Science News*, Vol. 92 (October 28, 1967), pp. 424–25.

*Ullman, Montague, and Krippner, Stanley, *Dream Studies and Telepathy*. New York, Parapsychology Foundation (paperback), 1970.

——— and Vaughan, Alan, *Dream Telepathy: An Experimental Odyssey*. New York, Macmillan, 1973.

Clairvoyance

Most of the books listed under "general" include this subject.

*Van Over, Raymond, *ESP and the Clairvoyants*. New York, Award Books (paperback), 1970.

Dowsing

Barrett, William, and Besterman, Theodore, *The Divining Rod: An Experimental and Psychological Investigation.* (c1926). New Hyde Park, N. Y., University Books, 1967. The classic on the subject.

Roberts, Kenneth, *Henry Gross and His Dowsing Rod.* Garden City, N. Y., Doubleday, 1951.

——— *The Seventh Sense.* Garden City, N. Y., Doubleday, 1953.

Precognition

Burgess, Anthony. "Precognition." *Playboy*, Vol. 19 (April, 1972), pp. 169–70.

Dunne, John W., *An Experiment with Time.* New York, Hillary, 1958.

*Ebon, Martin, *Prophecy in Our Time.* New York, New American Library, 1968. Out of print. Paperback: Borden Publishing Company.

*——— *True Experiences in Prophecy.* New York, New American Library, 1967. Out of print. Paperback: Signet.

Ellwood, Gracia-Fay, *Psychic Visits to the Past: An Exploration of Retrocognition.* New York, Signet (paperback), 1971.

*Garrett, Eileen, *The Sense and Nonsense of Prophecy.* New York, Creative Age Press, 1950. Out of print. Paperback: Medallion.

*Greenhouse, Herbert B., *Premonitions: A Leap into the Future.* New York, Bernard Geis Associates, 1971. Paperback: Warner Paperback Library.

Holzer, Hans, *Predictions: Fact or Fallacy.* New York, Hawthorn, 1968. Paperback: Crest.

Mihalsy, John, and others. "Dollars May Flow from the Sixth Sense: Precognition." *Nation's Business*, Vol. 59 (April, 1971), pp. 64–66.

Osborn, Arthur W., *The Future Is Now: The Significance of Precognition.* New Hyde Park, N. Y., University Books, 1962. Out of print. Paperback: Quest.

Vaughan, Alan, *Patterns of Prophecy.* New York, Hawthorn, 1972.

Psychokinesis

Rhine, Louisa E., *Mind Over Matter.* New York, Macmillan, 1970. Paperback: Macmillan-Collier.

Poltergeist

Bayless, Raymond, "The Poltergeist Meets the Law." *Psychic*, Vol. 5 (May–June, 1974), pp. 30–34.
*Knight, David C., *Poltergeists: Hauntings and the Haunted*. Philadelphia, Lippincott, 1972. Paperback: Weird and Horrible Library.
Rogo, D. Scott, "In Pursuit of the Poltergeist." *Psychic*, Vol. 5 (May–June, 1974), pp. 20–24.
*Roll, William G., *The Poltergeist*. Garden City, N. Y., Doubleday, 1973. Paperback: Signet.
See also "Kirlian Photography" under "Chapter 9."

New Frontiers in Parapsychology

Healing

Fuller, John G., *Arigo: Surgeon of the Rusty Knife*. New York, Crowell, 1974.
Hammond, Sally, *We Are All Healers*. New York, Harper and Row, 1973.
Montgomery, Ruth, *Born to Heal*. New York, Coward, McCann and Geoghegan, 1971. Paperback: Popular Library.
Sherman, Harold, *Your Power to Heal*. New York, Harper and Row, 1972.
Worrall, Ambrose and Olga, *The Gift of Healing*. 1965. Out of print. Paperback titled *The Miracle Healers*: Signet.

Kirlian Photography

Krippner, Stanley, and Rubin, Daniel, eds., *The Kirlian Aura: Photographing the Galaxies of Life*. 2d ed. Garden City, N. Y., Doubleday, 1974. Paperback: Anchor Books.
Rorvik, David M., "The Healing Hand of Mr. E." *Esquire*, Vol. 81 (February, 1974), pp. 70–71, 154–60. Estebany's aura.
Tiller, William, "Are Psychoenergetic Pictures Possible?" *New Scientist*, Vol. 62 (April 25, 1974), pp. 160–63.

Serios, Ted

Eisenbud, Jule, *The World of Ted Serios*. New York, Morrow, 1967. Paperback: Pocket Books.

Plants

Loehr, Franklin, *The Power of Prayer Over Plants*. New York, New American Library, 1969. Paperback: Signet.

Schwebs, Ursula, "Do Plants Have Feelings?" *Harper's Magazine*, Vol. 246 (June, 1973), pp. 75–76.

Tompkins, Peter, and Bird, Christopher, *The Secret Life of Plants*. New York, Harper and Row, 1973.

The Future

Survival of Death

Murphy, Gardner, *Three Papers on the Survival Problem*. New York, American Society for Psychical Research, 1969.

Myers, Frederic W. H., *Human Personality and Its Survival of Bodily Death*. (c1903). One-volume abridgement by Susy Smith: New Hyde Park, N. Y., University Books, 1961. Out of print. A classic treatment.

Pike, James A. (with Diane Kennedy), *The Other Side: An Account of My Experiences with Psychic Phenomena*. Garden City, N. Y., Doubleday, 1968.

Reincarnation

Bernstein, Morey, *The Search for Bridey Murphy*. (c1956). Rev. ed. Garden City, N. Y., Doubleday, 1965.

Ebon, Martin, ed., *Reincarnation in the 20th Century*. New York, World, 1969. Paperback: Signet.

Holzer, Hans, *Born Again: The Truth About Reincarnation*. Garden City, N. Y., Doubleday, 1970. Paperback: Pocket Books.

Leek, Sybil, *Reincarnation: The Second Chance*. New York, Stein and Day, 1974.

Stevenson, Ian, *Twenty Cases Suggestive of Reincarnation*. 2d. ed., Charlottesville, Va., University of Virginia Press, 1974. A classic study.

Out-of-Body Experiences (astral projection)

*Monroe, Robert A., *Journeys Out of the Body*. Garden City, N. Y., Doubleday, 1971. Paperback: Anchor Books.

Muldoon, Sylvan, and Carrington, Hereward, *The Phenomena of Astral Projection*. London, Rider, 1951. Paperback: Wehman.

——— *The Projection of the Astral Body*. Rev. ed. London, Rider, 1956. Paperbacks. Wehman.

Smith, Susy, *The Enigma of Out-of-Body Travel*. New York, Garrett-Helix, 1965. Paperback: Signet.

——— *Out-of-Body Experiences*. Los Angeles, Sherbourne Press (paperback), 1968.

Index